OUR KING
AND
QUEEN
AND THE
ROYAL
PRINCESSES

THEIR MAJESTIES KING GEORGE VI AND QUEEN ELIZABETH

OUR KING
AND QUEEN

AND THE

ROYAL
PRINCESSES

ODHAMS PRESS LTD, LONDON, W.C.2

[Photo from "Our Princesses and Their Dogs." Published by John Murray

THE ROYAL FAMILY AND THEIR PETS

HIS MAJESTY THE KING

DESTINY has had a strange fulfilment for Albert Frederick Arthur George, Prince of the Royal House of Windsor. Within eleven months he served two kings and became himself a king. Not very often have the pages of British history turned so swiftly and dramatically.

In January 1936, on the death of his father, George V, he became Heir to the Throne. Hardly had he laid aside the black cloth of mourning for his father than he was called upon to don himself the scarlet and ermine of the inherited Monarchy. In December he heard the trumpets sound in the ancient courtyard of St. James's Palace, and the voice of the King of Arms proclaim him King.

No King in history has ever ascended his Throne with a heavier and a sadder heart. No King has ever received a sterner call to duty. To have seen his brother, Edward VIII, sign away his Throne on the eve of his Coronation, to have heard the voice of this brother bid farewell to the Empire peoples, to have shaken his hand and to have watched him pass into voluntary exile—to have suffered thus is indeed a sad prelude to a Royal reign.

Yet his courage did not falter. With his beloved Queen and children at his side and confident of the loyalty and affection of his peoples, he took up the heavy burden of Kingship.

King George VI is the first Sovereign to be separately proclaimed King not only of the United Kingdom but of his Dominions Beyond the Seas. He is the King of Canada, South Africa, Australia and New Zealand. He is the Emperor of India. His rule unites desert, jungle, arctic wastes and coral-studded islands in Southern seas. The peoples of almost a quarter of the world's surface admit his rule.

Greater glory has been given to no Monarch since the world began. Yet he is humble in the shadow of this measure of power. To it all he brings a great spirit of democracy. As his kingship begins the trumpets sound their call, not to domination and infallible decree, but to Royal leadership of a great and free democracy.

In a speech he made long before he was conscious of the grave status and responsibility that was to be his, King George VI revealed much of his own code and character. Speaking of a leader of men he said, " To my mind he must possess three qualities : personality, sympathy and, above all, idealism. The man who wins the trust and confidence of his fellow-men so that they will follow him anywhere is the man who can combine in himself these three virtues."

There is a fourth quality in a leader which George VI has in full measure. That is courage. He fought at Jutland, the greatest sea battle of modern times. A frail, boyish figure, dogged by ill-health, he stuck to his post in the fore turret of the *Collingwood*, a member of the crew of a 12-inch gun. His ship was many times nearly struck during the engagement, and the young Prince was mentioned in despatches for his coolness under fire.

It can be said of him that he shares proudly the sailor traditions of his father, George V. Indeed, of all the brothers of the Royal family, he bears the closest resemblance to him.

His devotion to his Queen—still remembered as the smiling Duchess of York—and his love for his children, the two little Princesses, have at all times awakened responsive echoes among his people. To his Mother, Queen Mary, he has always been deeply attached, and the whole Empire rejoices that the Throne continues to be the symbol of contented hearth and home.

Many parts of the Empire already know him, for he has toured East Africa privately and, ten years ago, he went round the world after opening Australia's new city of Government. He crossed three oceans, travelled the length of Australia and New Zealand and made himself known and loved by British people in Polynesia, the East Indies and the Mediterranean.

King George VI has a keen sense of humour. He makes friends cautiously—but keeps them. He is a serious reader, and enjoys light music. He is a good swimmer and a fine horseman. The best athlete of the Royal family, he played in the Men's Tennis Doubles at Wimbledon in 1926, is a good golfer, and can hold his own in the polo field.

At forty-one, George VI takes public life seriously. Quietly and modestly he has displayed a considerable interest in industry. His devotion even to the most irksome duty, his keenness for facts, his memory for faces, his respect for tradition will hold him in good stead in the years to come. " You may rest assured that it is my determination to do all that lies within my power to safeguard the liberties of my people and promote their prosperity and contentment," he declared in a first message to Parliament.

Many years ago the King inaugurated his now famous "Duke of York's" summer camp for boys drawn from the public schools and from industrial firms. It was an experiment that succeeded, a gesture of practical democracy. Year after year His Majesty spent at least one night under canvas with the lads, sang with them around the camp fire, talked with them, played with them, and understood them.

Co-operation between all classes has always been his watchword. "One of the great needs of to-day," he said at Melbourne, "and perhaps the greatest need of all, is the better understanding of one another, both between the different parts of the Empire and also between the different interests—Capital and Labour, employers and employed, town and country—in the various countries themselves." Over and over again he has lived up to his part as illustrated in those words. And so he will go on. The British King has, to an exceptional degree, to combine service with leadership. For that task, George VI is excellently prepared.

His 34,000 mile tour of Australia and New Zealand in 1927 proved him to be a competent and popular ambassador of the Mother Country. At home, too, he and Queen Elizabeth have rendered invaluable public service.

King George VI was born at York Cottage, Sandringham. To him Sandringham has always been Home. It is here that His Majesty and Queen Elizabeth, the little Princesses, Queen Mary and other members of the Royal family will gather on many occasions during the long and peaceful reign that the whole Empire prays they may enjoy for many long and peaceful years to come.

King George VI faces a future that may hold much to test and burden him. None can predict the lights and shadows of history's kaleidoscope. One thing is certain: that as the guns crash their salutes from park and tower, as the bells echo their peals of praise, he and Queen Elizabeth will be accorded the unstinted affection and good wishes and loyalty of the whole British Commonwealth of Nations.

George V was a successful monarch because he remained loyal to his peoples at all times. His judgment never betrayed him or them.

The prestige of the monarchy was raised to great heights by him. It is the task of King George VI and his Queen to keep it high. Who can doubt that this couple, young as years go, but backed by the soundest experience, will succeed? With them, because of them, and through them the great principle of democracy will be made to live— that the united desires of the people must and will prevail.

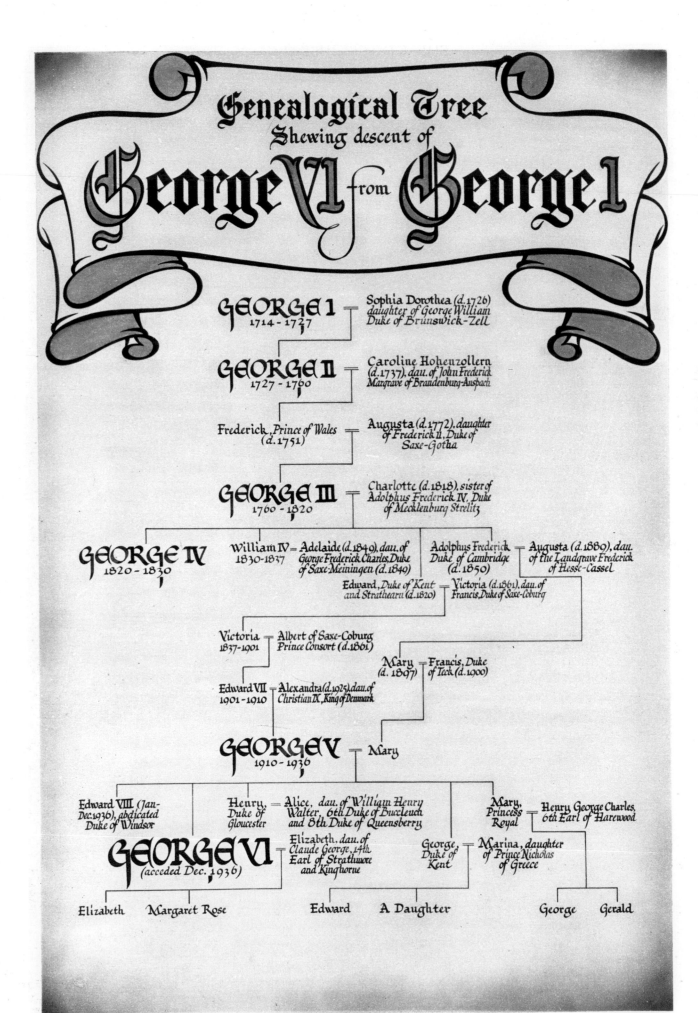

Genealogical Tree
Shewing descent of
George VI from George I

GEORGE I 1714-1727 — Sophia Dorothea (d.1726) daughter of George William Duke of Brunswick-Zell

GEORGE II 1727-1760 — Caroline Hohenzollern (d.1737), dau. of John Frederick Margrave of Brandenburg-Anspach

Frederick, Prince of Wales (d.1751) — Augusta (d.1772), daughter of Frederick II, Duke of Saxe-Gotha

GEORGE III 1760-1820 — Charlotte (d.1818), sister of Adolphus Frederick IV, Duke of Mecklenburg Strelitz

GEORGE IV 1820-1830

William IV 1830-1837 = Adelaide (d.1849), dau. of George Frederick Charles, Duke of Saxe-Meiningen (d.1849)

Adolphus Frederick Duke of Cambridge (d.1850) — Augusta (d.1889), dau. of the Landgrave Frederick of Hesse-Cassel

Edward, Duke of Kent and Strathearn (d.1820) — Victoria (d.1861), dau. of Francis, Duke of Saxe-Coburg

Victoria 1837-1901 — Albert of Saxe-Coburg Prince Consort (d.1861)

Mary (d.1897) — Francis, Duke of Teck (d.1900)

Edward VII 1901-1910 — Alexandra (d.1925), dau. of Christian IX, King of Denmark

GEORGE V 1910-1936 — Mary

Edward VIII (Jan-Dec.1936), abdicated Duke of Windsor

Henry, Duke of Gloucester = Alice, dau. of William Henry Walter, 6th Duke of Buccleuch and 8th Duke of Queensberry

Mary, Princess Royal — Henry George Charles, 6th Earl of Harewood

GEORGE VI (acceded Dec., 1936) — Elizabeth, dau. of Claude George, 14th Earl of Strathmore and Kinghorne

George, Duke of Kent — Marina, daughter of Prince Nicholas of Greece

Elizabeth   Margaret Rose   Edward   A Daughter   George   Gerald

At York Cottage, Sandringham, where Queen Victoria had assembled her family for Christmas, Prince Albert, second son of the Duke and Duchess of York was born on December 14, 1895. It was almost exactly forty-one years later, on the abdication of his brother Edward VIII, that he succeeded to the throne under the style of George VI.

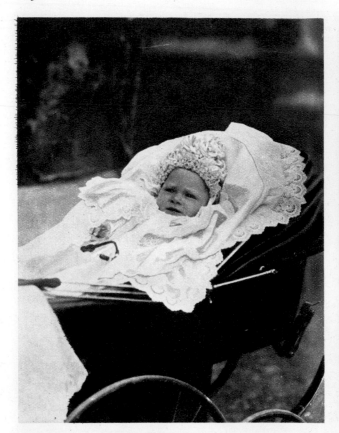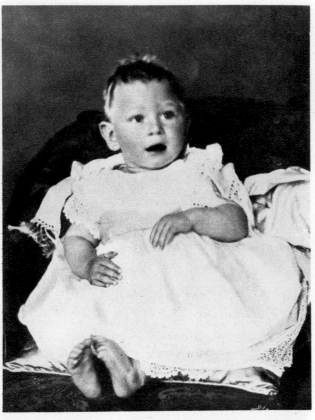

Prince Albert was born in that happy period when the Duke and Duchess were permitted by light State duties to live an uninterrupted family life. The picture on the left shows him as a young baby and (*right*) at the age of nine months. The nursery was under the charge of " Mrs. Bill," who later became housekeeper at Buckingham Palace.

The Church of St. Mary Magdalene at Sandringham is the place of worship of the royal family while in Norfolk. Here the new Prince was christened by the then Bishop of Norwich, Albert Frederick Arthur George; and here, forty years later, his father lay in state and then began that series of events which brought his second son to the throne.

These charming portraits were taken when Prince Albert was about two years old. Sixteen months after Prince Albert, Princess Mary was born, giving joy to the Duke and Duchess of York, who wished for a daughter. On the left is the first picture of the three Royal children. Prince Albert is on the right and the infant Princess Mary lies in front.

White Lodge, Richmond Park, was the first residence of the Duke and Duchess of York. Frogmore House, in Windsor Park, was another of Prince Albert's homes, especially when the Queen was at Windsor. A royal residence since the time of George III, the house (seen from across the lake), stands in lovely surroundings not far from Windsor Castle.

Osborne House, in the Isle of Wight, was a favourite residence of Queen Victoria and frequently housed gatherings of relatives and friends. This interesting group which was photographed in the summer of this year shows Queen Victoria in the centre with the Duke of York and Prince Albert on her right. The Duchess of York is third from

the left with Princess Mary on her knee and Prince Edward at her side. Prince Arthur of Connaught stands with his hand on the back of the Queen's chair. Included in the group are Princess Ena of Battenburg, afterwards Queen of Spain, Princess Patricia of Connaught, Princess Victoria of York and Princess Margaret of Connaught.

Before she died, Queen Victoria saw one more grandchild added to the little group in which she was so keenly interested and which included two future kings of England. Prince Henry was born on March 31, 1900, and is in the Queen's arms in this picture. Prince Albert sits in front of Princess Mary, who has Prince Edward on her left.

Lady Elizabeth Bowes Lyon, now Queen of England, fourth and youngest daughter of the Earl and Countess of Strathmore, was born on August 4, 1900, at St. Paul's, Waldenbury, near Hitchin, the beautiful English home of her Scottish father. With six brothers and three sisters, she began here a happy, sunny childhood.

When Prince Albert's parents became Prince and Princess of Wales, it was necessary to have a home in London owing to a vast increase in duties, and Marlborough House, built by Wren in 1710, was chosen. After King Edward's death, Queen Alexandra lived there, and twenty-six years later Queen Mary returned to Marlborough House as Queen Mother.

King Edward, who was devoted to his grandchildren, took a great interest in their doings, and, as far as was possible, arranged for them to spend their holidays with him. This picture was taken during the annual autumn visit of the King to Balmoral when Prince Albert (*right*) was about seven years old and the young Prince Henry, two.

This snapshot of the Duke of York was taken while he was staying in the country and shows him with his family and a pet dog. Prince Henry is holding his father's hand and Prince Albert is on the left of the group. About this time, the Duchess of York retired from public life for a while and the fourth son, Prince George, was born.

Riding is as much a part of a Prince's education as book learning, and all the children of the Duke and Duchess of York began at a very early age to accustom themselves to the saddle. The picture above shows the young Princes Albert and Edward riding in Windsor Park in the charge of a groom. Sailor Suits persisted even on horseback.

Glamis Castle, the ancient home of the Earls of Strathmore, is said to be the oldest inhabited house in the British Isles. King Malcolm II died of wounds in a room known to-day as Malcolm's Room. Macbeth was a Thane of Glamis; Patrick Lyon was hostage for James I and, when the '45 began, the Strathmores were wholehearted Jacobites.

There is a Prince Charlie Room and a Scott Room in this grand old feudal keep, standing midway between the Grampians and the Sidlaws in the fertile plain known as the " Howe of Strathmore." Inset is a picture of the Queen as a little girl walking with her father on the Castle cricket ground where many famous matches have been played.

The Queen grew up in a household, whether in Hertfordshire or Scotland, where children ruled. A vast collection of pets, beautiful gardens, the squabbles and ecstatic enthusiasms of early years, combined to give her a childhood of rare happiness and a natural unspoiled charm. The picture is from a miniature done when she was six years old.

Dancing was a delight to the Queen as a child. With her brother David, she loved to raid the family chest of old costumes and to " dress up " for the minuet in which she acquitted herself so well. This picture shows them with their dancing master on such an occasion. The children also took private lessons at the Sun Hotel, in Hitchin, Hertfordshire.

There were none of the necessary insistences on rank and future in the Queen's upbringing. On her native heath in Scotland, she roamed like her brothers and sisters, a child of the country, and looking almost sorry for herself when, as on the left of this photograph, she was dressed up in formal garden-party clothes for a fête at Glamis Castle.

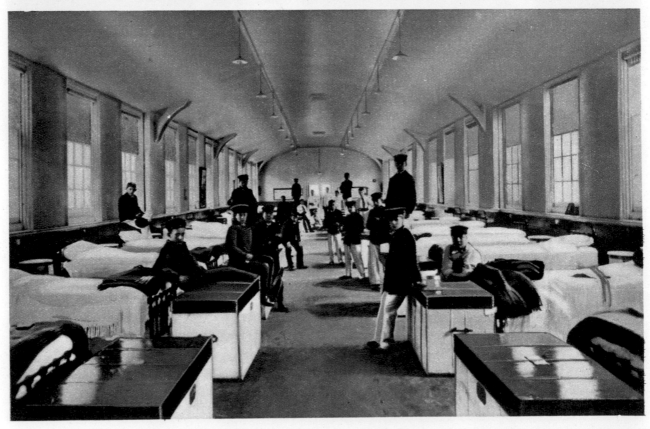

Dormitories at Osborne, where Prince Albert went to begin a naval career, were much like those of any boarding school, except that sea-chests replaced trunks at the foot of the beds. Prince Albert lived entirely as the other cadets in a typical school atmosphere stiffened by Service discipline and the concentration of training for one career.

Prince Albert followed two years after his elder brother to Osborne, and is seen as a cadet in the left-hand picture. On the right are King George's family at his accession. Prince Albert was nearly fifteen years old and had been training for a year at Osborne. The picture shows him on the left behind Prince John, who was born in 1905.

Seven monarchs walked in the funeral procession of Edward VII, which is shown here entering Windsor Castle for the interment in the Chapel Royal. George V walked between the Kaiser, on his right, and the Duke of Connaught. Prince Albert is behind the Duke, with his eldest brother. On the left of the picture is ex-King Alfonso of Spain.

Balmoral Castle, the home of the royal family in Scotland, was built by the Prince Consort in 1848. Afterwards, Edward VII and George V both used the Castle for autumn holidays and for the shooting. The very extensive estate covers 24,000 acres, much of which is deer forest, and the beautiful River Dee flows past the Castle grounds.

The children of the Prince and Princess of Wales were very fond of Balmoral, for the Castle in the Scottish Highlands was a home where they could run wild for a short time. When this picture was taken, Prince Albert was nearly fifteen and Prince Henry, on his left, five years younger. Prince George now growing fast, was eight years old.

When Edward VII came to the throne, the education of Prince Edward was entrusted to Mr. Hansell, an outstanding man both physically and mentally. In due course, Prince Albert, too, became his charge. During holidays from Dartmouth, he "crammed" for his examinations with Mr. Hansell. Here they are walking in the grounds of Balmoral in the autumn of the year King Edward VII died. By virtue of this sad fact, Prince Albert was now second in succession to the throne.

Early in 1911, both Prince Albert and his brother caught measles at Dartmouth and they were both of them, sent to Newquay to complete their convalescence. Mr. Hansell introduced them to golf, and days on the bracing Cornish links soon gave them back their health.

On June 22, George V, father of Prince Albert, was crowned in Westminster Abbey and the picture shows his glittering coach entering the courtyard of Buckingham Palace after the ceremony. Prince Albert rode with Princess Mary and two of his younger brothers in a State coach and the solemn occasion could not check their youthful levity.

In the dim quietness of the Abbey, Prince Albert saw the ancient ceremony beginning with words which were to be his almost exactly twenty-six years later : " Sirs; I here present unto you King George, the undoubted King of this realm. Wherefore all of you who are come this day to do your homage and service, are you willing to do the same?"

Dartmouth College, the great training centre for naval officers, attended by both Prince Albert and his elder brother, is a modern building, high above the beautiful estuary at Dartmouth. It was opened in 1905, and, after entrance by competitive examination, boys usually remain there for a four-years' course. It accommodates about 500 boys.

Visits from parents and relations are as welcome at a Naval College as at any other school. The picture shows the Princes Albert and Edward during a visit from their mother's brother, Alexander, Prince of Teck, who was later created Earl of Athlone. Prince Edward passed out of Dartmouth during this year, but his brother's training lasted for a further twelve months.

Cadets who had finished shore training at Dartmouth usually went to sea for an extensive cruise to get practical experience of navigation before becoming midshipmen. Prince Albert duly took his cruise, and the picture shows him driving to Devonport with a large batch of fellow cadets to embark for the cadet cruise of his year.

At this time, Lady Elizabeth Bowes Lyon was thirteen years of age and fast acquiring a reputation as a young hostess in Scotland and Hertfordshire. It is said of her that some guests were more shy than she was, and that she would make a point of engaging each in a few minutes quiet talk which soon put them at their ease.

Scenic railways were a new invention then and provided one of the sensations of the Earls Court Exhibition. Prince Albert insisted on trying its fearful joys. In this photograph Princess Mary seems apprehensive of the next drop, but Prince Albert, perhaps with the calm which has made him so good an airman, is anticipating it with pleasure.

Prince Albert was a midshipman in the gun-room of H.M.S. *Collingwood*, at the historic review of the Fleet at Spithead this summer. He is seen examining through his telescope the twenty-two miles of warships which, fresh from a visit to the German naval base at Kiel, were destined never to separate except to go to war stations a short month later.

Illness dogged Prince Albert after the beginning of the war, in which he served as a Naval officer. Following appendicitis, he rejoined H.M.S. *Collingwood*, only to be sent ashore with internal trouble. While undergoing treatment, he assisted in war work and, in the picture (*right*) is pouring out tea for the wounded at Buckingham Palace.

Prince Albert's ship was in the First Battle Squadron on duty at Scapa Flow as soon as war was declared. H.M.S. *Collingwood* (*above*, was a battleship carrying ten 12-inch guns. Although not hit at Jutland, she was in the thick of the battle and had many narrow escapes. Prince Albert was mentioned in dispatches for coolness under fire.

During 1916, two tragic events affected the Strathmore family. First came the news that Lady Elizabeth's brother Fergus had been killed at Loos, and, at the end of the year, a serious fire threatened Glamis Castle. These pictures, taken during the war, show the Queen as she then was. On the right, she is with her father, the Earl of Strathmore.

When the dreadful stream of wounded began to return from France, Glamis Castle was converted into a hospital. The ancient walls witnessed anew the effects of warfare, while the bracing air healed the men they housed. Lady Elizabeth and the Countess of Strathmore are seen here with a group of convalescent wounded during that time.

The effects of operations following on his illness prevented Prince Albert from pursuing his naval career. He thereupon joined the newest fighting service, the Royal Naval Air Service. This picture of him preparing for a flight was taken at the time when the Royal Naval Air Service amalgamated with the Flying Corps and became the Royal Air Force.

Prince Albert went to the air station at Cranwell in February of the last year of the war. Here he is shown carrying out a routine inspection in the Cadet Brigade where he remained for eight months. He then was promoted to the staff of Sir Hugh Trenchard and went to the Western Front, moving into Belgium after the Armistice in 1918.

[Photo: Imperial War Museum

Belgium was at last regained from the hands of the invader, and, on November 22, King Albert entered Brussels at the head of a triumphant army. Prince Albert represented his father and Belgium's British allies. He is seen here as they entered the city, riding between the King of the Belgians and the boy Prince Charles at the head of the cavalcade.

[Photo: Imperial War Museum

In December following the Armistice, King George V made a short victory tour through the shattered fields of France and Belgium, accompanied by his two elder sons. They are shown in the streets of Stambruges with cheering townspeople and soldiers on either side. Prince Albert is next to the Prince of Wales, who is on his father's right.

Prince Albert remained in Belgium under service conditions till February of the next year, when he went to the Air Ministry in England. The above portrait was taken about this time. While at the Ministry, he began flying at Waddon Aerodrome and took his certificate in due course. The inset picture shows his machine in flight during this training.

The National Rifle Association held their meeting at Bisley in July.   Prince Albert presented the prizes.   In the picture, Lord Cheylemore is pointing out features of the ranges.   The N.R.A. has the distinction of having had a member of the Royal Family present at every meeting since the first shot was fired by Queen Victoria in 1860.

Troops from all the victorious armies assembled in London on July 19 and, with colours crowned with laurels, marched through the streets and along the Mall where the King and Queen waited.   On the steps of the Victoria Memorial, a pavilion had been erected and here King and Queen and Princes and other eminent notabilities greeted the fighting men.

Prince Albert had been prevented by the War from going to a university. In October, however, Prince Henry was going up and his brother accompanied him. They rented a house in Southacre, and Wing-Commander Louis Greig and his wife kept house for them. Commander Greig is on the right in this picture of the Princes taken in Cambridge.

Like all undergraduates, Prince Albert possessed a bicycle for the daily journeys to and from the College. But, for longer trips, he had the motor-cycle on which he is riding here. The next year was to see him enter fully into public life while the Prince of Wales was away on his Canadian tour and he could only remain a little while at the University.

In November, the President of France, Monsieur Poincaré, paid a state visit to England. Prince Albert was chosen to welcome officially the head of a country which had been fighting with Britain less than a year before. This picture shows Monsieur Poincaré and Prince Albert leaving the Guildhall after a State Drive with an escort to the City.

Soon after a triumphant tour in Canada, the Prince of Wales left England to visit Australasia. Prince Albert and Prince Henry travelled down to Portsmouth to bid him farewell, and this picture was taken aboard H.M.S. *Renown*. On the right is Lord Louis Mountbatten, the Princes' cousin, then a sub-lieutenant serving on the battle cruiser.

(Photo: Lafayette

One of Lady Elizabeth Bowes Lyon's brothers was killed in the Great War and another returned ill from a German prison camp. But the family was now together again, and Glamis Castle no longer a hospital. At this time, Lady Elizabeth appeared at functions in London. At one of these she met Prince Albert for the first time since childhood.

[Photo: Vandyk]

A Prince of the royal blood has no seat in the House of Lords. It was not until he was created Duke of York in the Birthday Honours of King George V this year that Prince Albert was able to sit in the House. He was sponsored on June 23 by the Duke of Connaught and the Duke of Northumberland, and is seen robed for the ceremony.

41

In July, the Duke went to a fete at Bexley in aid of an ex-Service Men's club, where he is shown enthusiastically throwing at the Aunt Sally. The picture on the right shows him at the time he won the Doubles Championships of the Royal Air Force at Queen's Club with Wing-Commander Greig against the best players in the Service.

Another movement with which the Duke of York has identified himself is the Boy Scout Movement. Here, the Duke is seen sitting to the left of Lord Baden-Powell, founder of the movement, at a Scouts' Rally held in Cannon Hill Park, Birmingham, in July. They are watching a march past of Wolf Cubs, which was a feature of the great Jamboree.

[Photo: Benwell Latchmore

This interesting group was taken at the Hertfordshire home of the Earl of Strathmore.   Between Lady Elizabeth on the left and her mother stands the young Prince Paul of Yugoslavia, who became Regent of his country in 1934.   The Hon. David Bowes Lyon, Lady Elizabeth's youngest brother and inseparable companion, is seated in front.

Armistice Day this year, the second since war ended, was notable for two outstanding events. First, the permanent Cenotaph in Whitehall, designed by Sir Edwin Lutyens, was unveiled by King George V, and, afterwards, came the most poignant memorial to the cruelty and futility of war—the burial of the Unknown Warrior. Flanked by the

marching figures of great commanders, the coffin passed down Whitehall. Behind it walked the King, behind him the Prince of Wales, the Duke of York, Prince Henry and the Duke of Connaught. Then came the Ministers of the Crown and members of both Houses with troops of Empire to many of whom this unknown dead soldier might have been comrade.

In June, Lord Birkenhead organised a tennis party at his country
home, Charlton, near Banbury.
The Duke of York, after having
been a spectator at several tennis
meetings, now enjoyed active
participation to the full. He is
a steady lefthander, and the
picture shows him taking a back-
hand return from a hard service.

The event of the tennis week-
end at Lord Birkenhead's home
was a match against the Oxford
University team. The Duke of
York is here discussing a
game with his opponents.
Tennis was played under ideal
conditions, with no tournament
cares and in perfect weather.

This picture of Lady Elizabeth was taken just after she attained her majority. A shadow was cast over her family from early spring by the serious illness of her mother, the Countess of Strathmore. During these anxious months, Lady Elizabeth acted in her place and became the chatelaine of the great castle at Glamis and a notable hostess.

Although Lady Elizabeth had met the Duke once as a child and again at a social function in London, the link between the two families was at first formed by Princess Mary. As an officer of the Girl Guides, the Princess had become very friendly with Lady Elizabeth, who had similar interests. The picture (*below*) shows a part of the beautiful drawing-room at Glamis Castle.

[*Photo: Hoppé*

A football match in aid of the Dockland Settlement and Malburn Boys' Club, Canning Town, was arranged during the autumn. The Corinthians played the 'Spurs on the Tottenham ground and lost by two goals to one. The Duke of York kicked off before an enthusiastic crowd, who saw to it that the Settlement benefited by a large sum.

The British Empire Exhibition at Wembley, planned to open two years later, really began when the Duke of York cut the first sod on the chosen site. The turf selected was on the exact spot over which the King would pass when he drove in state to open the Exhibition, the greatest that the British Empire, and probably the world, had ever known.

[Photo: W. and D. Downey

On February 28, Princess Mary was married to Viscount Lascelles, later Earl of Harewood. The ceremony was performed in Westminster Abbey and Lady Elizabeth Bowes Lyon was one of the bridesmaids. This group taken at the time, shows, left to right, the Duke of York, Queen Mary, Prince George and Prince Henry.

The Duke attended the football match between English and Scottish schoolboys at Stamford Bridge in May, an event the popularity of which increased each year. He is seen shaking hands with the Scottish captain before the game. He presented caps to both teams before play began. A crowd of 25,000 cheered an English victory after a very even game.

The Middlesex Hospital, which was now in great need of modern buildings, and the Industrial Welfare Society, were jointly benefited by a motor-cycle meeting at Brooklands in late May. The Duke entered his own machine in several races and it was ridden by the famous motor-cyclist, S. E. Wood, to whom the Duke is here seen talking.

A picture, taken at Glamis Castle, which shows Lady Elizabeth Bowes Lyon talking to Mr. Gavin Ralston, Factor of the Estate.   Since Princess Mary's wedding, she had frequently been seen dancing with the Duke of York, and already it was beginning to be rumoured that an engagement might be announced.   The rumour later proved true.

In July, the Brigade of Guards received new colours from the hands of King George V at a brilliant ceremony.   The picture above was taken during the march past immediately afterwards.   Behind the Duke of York, who is in the dress uniform of the Royal Air Force, is the Prince of Wales. The presentation took place on the Horse Guards' Parade.

During a visit to Cambridge, the Honorary Degree of Doctor of Law was conferred upon the Duke at the University. Mr. Taft, ex-president, and then Chief Justice, of the United States, received the honour at the same time, and is seen walking second from the left of the gowned figures in the picture.

The Duke was in the saddle again during August, when he went to Spring Hill Farm, near Rugby, to stay with the Hon. F. E. Guest. A week's polo had been arranged and the picture shows the Duke coming on to the field for the match, in which Templeton played Hillmorton.

This unconventional study of Lady Elizabeth Bowes Lyon was taken during a shoot at Glamis. Though never a keen shot, Lady Elizabeth loved any sport that took her to the woods and hills around the great castle. But the day was near when new responsibilities and position would increasingly rob her of leisure.

Amongst the few pictures showing the Duke of York and Lady Elizabeth Bowes Lyon together before they were engaged is this group taken at Glamis Castle during this autumn. The Duke is seen standing behind Lady Elizabeth and between the Hon. David Bowes Lyon, on his right, and the Earl of Strathmore.

The fourth Armistice Day came and England's millions observed it solemnly. Thought was concentrated on the white Cenotaph in London where King and people kept the Silence. In the picture are shown King George V with his eldest sons, the Duke of York in the foreground, the Prince of Wales beside him, during the impressive quiet.

[Photo: Vandyk

During January, Lady Elizabeth Bowes Lyon was at St. Paul's Waldenbury, and the Duke of York went to stay there on the 13th. The proposal was made in the romantic wood of her childhood and, on January 16 the *Court Circular* announced the engagement, to which " the King has gladly given his consent and which everybody welcomed."

For many years, King George V spent Easter at Windsor Castle and this year was no exception.   For once, all his sons were together, and this picture of them was secured during the holiday.   They ride with King George on the left, the Prince of Wales next to him, then the Duke of York, Prince Henry and Prince George in order of their birth.

The recreational side of business and industrial houses always appealed strongly to the Duke.   In early April he attended the final round of the Insurance Companies' Football Cup, and is here shown shaking hands with the Motor Union team before the match, which was played against Cuaco and resulted in much entertaining football.

During the three months between the announcement of the engagement and their marriage, the Duke and Lady Elizabeth Bowes Lyon met frequently. Too often there were the formal details of a State wedding to be settled, but, on occasions, the couple left the Earl of Strathmore's London home, as in this picture, for private shopping expeditions.

On April 26, bride and retinue came to Westminster Abbey where so many historic marriages have been solemnised, and where the bridegroom waited. Here they kneel before the Archbishop of Canterbury. King George, Queen Mary, Queen Alexandra, the Princes, stand all around. And outside the people wait to give their greeting.

The Duke of York was married in the full dress of the Royal Air Force. His bride's dress was of ivory chiffon moiré, with pearl embroideries on cloth of silver and a panel of silver falling between the shoulders to gleam through the veil. On the left of the picture are the Earl and Countess of Strathmore and Kinghorne, the bride's father and mother.

King George and Queen Mary are on the right with their son. To pose for this picture was the last State duty of the wedding. Now it was no longer a popular spectacle and Duke and Duchess were free to be with their families in private celebration. After an appearance on the balcony of the Palace which the crowd applauded enthusiastically.

After a short time, the newly-married couple appeared again, dressed for the journey, the bride now in dove-grey. Princes and bridesmaids bombarded them with rose petals as they drove out of the Palace archway on their way to Polesden Lacey, a beautiful house at Bookham, in Surrey, lent for the honeymoon by the Hon. Mrs. Ronald Greville.

The Duke and Duchess spent their short time at Polesden Lacey walking in the country and playing golf. They then went to Glamis Castle till the end of May and came South again to spend a last fortnight at Frogmore. By that time, their home, White Lodge, Richmond, the preparation of which had been supervised by Queen Mary, was ready for them.

The Royal Air Force Pageant at Hendon Aerodrome takes place at the end of June. Becoming every year a more amazing and more entertaining display, it was honoured this year by the presence of the Duke and Duchess. The recently-married couple were given a tumultuous reception when they arrived. The picture shows them going to their seats.

The Royal Air Force Memorial on the Victoria Embankment in London was unveiled by the Prince of Wales on July 16. The Duke of York attended him as a high officer of the Service, and is here seen with his brother and Lord Trenchard, with whom he served in France, as they walk to the Memorial past the guard of honour at the salute.

When the annual outing of the Fresh Air Fund was held in Epping Forest, the Duke and Duchess spent several hours with the thousand poor children taken there for a precious day in the open. The Duchess tried her skill at the coconut shies, and it is pleasant to relate that, two seconds after this picture was taken, she knocked over a " milky one."

This group shows the Royal Family when King George V was fifty-eight years of age and had been twelve years on the throne. The Duke of York and Princess Mary had each recently married, Princess Mary in 1922 and the Duke of York in the April of this year. The first grandchild of the family had been born in February to the Princess.

President Harding of the United States of America died in tragic circumstances in August and the Duke of York represented King George at a Memorial Service in Westminster Abbey. The picture above shows him leaving after the Service, which attracted to the Abbey many Americans staying in England and hundreds of other mourners.

Ever since their honeymoon, the Duke and Duchess had had an incessant round of formal engagements and social duties and were in need of rest. They went to Glamis Castle and then spent some days at Balmoral, where this picture was taken. It shows, left to right, Prince George, the Duchess and Duke of York, and Queen Mary, starting for a walk.

Princess Maud was married to Lord Carnegie in November, and this picture was taken as the couple left for the honeymoon. The Prince of Wales is on the left behind Prince Henry. On the steps are Queen Alexandra, Queen Mary and a bridesmaid. King George V is next to his youngest son Prince George, and the Duke of York on the extreme right.

Three Princes attended the Army Point to Point Meeting at Arborfield Cross, Wokingham. The Duke of York is seen between his two brothers, the Prince of Wales and Prince Henry, both of whom were riding. In the racing for Lord Cavan's Cup, the Prince of Wales fell heavily and was carried from the field with concussion and abrasions of the face.

Riding played a large part in the family's recreation at Easter, which was spent at Windsor. In the picture, King George V is riding with Viscount Lascelles. The Duke of York follows behind between Prince Henry, on his right, and Prince George. Soon after the Easter holiday the Duke and Duchess moved from Richmond to Chesterfield House.

The vast project at Wembley, begun when the Duke of York cut the first turf two years before, came to fruition on St. George's Day. On that day, King George V and Queen Mary and their family drove in State to the gigantic Exhibition of Empire that now awaited its opening. The Prince of Wales received them as President of the Exhibition, and asked

the King to perform the ceremony. The picture brings back the scene at the moment of opening. The Duke of York stands on his father's right. Farther away, between the pillars, Princess Mary can be seen. She is standing between her husband, Viscount Lascelles, and her brother Prince Henry, who is in Hussar's uniform, with a tall plume.

The dockland districts of London through which flows so much of Britain's trade, welcomed the Duke and Duchess late in April. The picture shows the Duchess receiving the key with which she opened the new Dockland Settlement Club in Canning Town. Afterwards, both the Duke and Duchess had tea with local children.

A less formal visit was paid to Wembley in May, and the Duke and Duchess spent some time in the Amusement Park with the Prince of Wales. This delightful picture was taken as the party started for a breath-taking ride on the Giant Switchback. All the Royal party emphatically announced their intention of visiting the Park again.

[Photo: Vandyk

In honour of the King and Queen of Rumania, who came to England this year on a visit, a State Ball was held at Buckingham Palace on May 14. Two thousand guests were present, among them were many distinguished foreign visitors, diplomats, and soldiers. This portrait of the Duke and Duchess shows them in full dress for the occasion.

Ras Tafari, Prince Regent of Ethiopia, visited England in July. After a civic reception at Dover, the Duke of York greeted him at Victoria. The Regent saw King George V and the Prime Minister, and visited Wembley before he returned to the country from which, as the Emperor Haile Selassie, the Italians drove him twelve years later.

During the summer, a great Jamboree was held at Wembley at which Boy Scouts from nearly every country in the world were present. The picture shows the Duke of York with Lord Baden-Powell, the Chief Scout, nearest the camera, watching with keen interest a display in the great Stadium after opening a special day for Wolf Cubs.

The Duke added to his experience of driving during a visit to Glasgow in September. He opened a new recreation ground for the employees of the Corporation Tramways Department and afterwards, to the huge delight of the thousands of cheering spectators, he drove a tram for more than a mile through the crowded streets to the depot.

[Photo: The Times

The Duke and Duchess began an African journey on December 5. It was a private tour and respected as such by the newspapers. There were a few official duties during the course of the holiday such as the visit to King Daudi of Buganda, which is shown here. Members of the Native Parliament promised loyalty and there was a grand review of warriors.

This visit to the Makwar Irrigation Dam across the Blue Nile was another official occasion. Before they embarked for the voyage to England again, the Duke and Duchess had toured Kenya, Uganda and Tanganyika, had enjoyed first-class big-game hunting, and had voyaged down the Nile through the Sudan and Egypt and so to Suez, Marseilles and home.

The Guest Hospital at Dudley, Worcestershire, has an extensive children's section, some of whose patients are seen here in the sunshine when the Duke and Duchess of York visited the hospital. At a bazaar, the Duke drove a miniature train, and had among his passengers Lord and Lady Ednam, and the Mayor and Mayoress of the borough.

This charming group was taken in the Stadium of the British Empire Exhibition at Wembley in June. It shows the Duke and Duchess making friends with some of the competitors in the Sheep Dog Trials. The proceedings were enlivened by two sheep which eluded the keen vigilance of the dogs and enjoyed their short freedom to the full.

The Prince of Wales had been away for seven months on an Imperial Tour and, on October 16, he returned in triumph to Portsmouth. The Duke and Prince Henry and the Guard of Honour were soaked as they waited on the quayside in the rain for H.M.S. *Repulse* to dock, but this delightful picture well shows their pleasure at the Prince's return.

At the end of October, the British Empire Exhibition closed its doors after providing the Empire and the World with one of the greatest displays of industry and art ever known. The Duke, accompanied by the Duchess performed the ceremony. The picture shows the presentation of a casket of cigarettes to the Duke before the closing luncheon.

On a grey, cold day, with snowflakes quietly falling, Queen Alexandra, mother of George V and beloved grandmother of his children, was buried. This picture of the procession to Westminster Abbey shows King George V between the Prince of Wales, on his right, and the Crown Prince Olaf of Norway. Behind them walk the Duke of York and Prince Henry.

A daughter was born to the Duke and Duchess on April 21. There were no setbacks in the baby's progress or the Mother's recovery, and the christening was arranged for a little more than a month ahead. The picture shows the Duchess leaving for the service with the baby Princess in the nurse's arms.

The Archbishop of York performed the ceremony and the little gold font was brought from the Chapel Royal at Windsor. The god-parents were King George V and Queen Mary, Princess Mary, the Duke of Connaught and the Earl and Countess of Strathmore. They are all seen in this group taken after the service. The lady on the extreme left is Lady Elphinstone, a sister of the Duchess of York.

Another picture taken at the time of the christening showing the Duke and Duchess with the baby Princess Elizabeth. The robe used at the christening was of Brussels lace, and had been worn before by the children of Queen Victoria, Queen Alexandra, Queen Mary, and by Princess Mary's little son. Water from the Jordan was used in the font.

The Duke entered for the Doubles Championship at Wimbledon this year with Wing-Commander Louis Greig. This picture, taken during the game, shows the Duke smashing a high return, and his partner, Wing-Commander Louis Greig, standing by. They played those wily veterans A. W. Gore and H. Roper Barrett, who won after an exciting game.

Early in January the Duke and Duchess left for Australia on an official visit to open the new Parliament Buildings at Canberra. They sailed on H.M.S. *Renown*, and this picture taken at the moment of departure, shows the Prince of Wales kissing his sister-in-law good-bye. Prince Henry is in the background, and the Duke of York to his right.

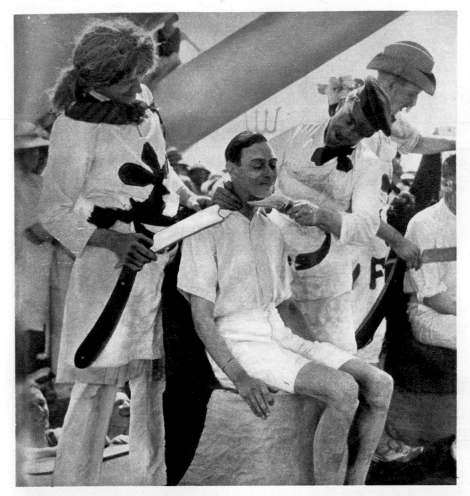

On February 2, *Renown* crossed the Line. The officers refused to accept the Duke's plea that he had crossed before on the liner going to Africa and he suffered all the warship ceremonial. In the picture, the Giant Razor waits to complete the work of Neptune's distemper brush, after which he will be granted the title of Old Sea Dog.

The King of the Sea and his fantastic henchmen then turned their attentions to the Duchess. She enjoyed a less exacting form of initiation, being touched on the forehead with equatorial sea water and presented ceremonially with the Order of the Golden Mermaid. The latter was a brass figure worked on board.

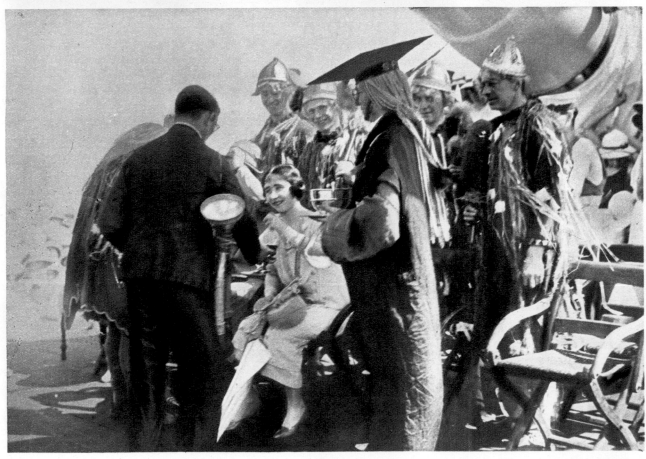

A ceremonial during a call at Suva, in Fiji, was the preparation of Yagona by the natives for the Duke of York to "drink himself in" as paramount chief. The Duke was the third of his house to perform the ceremony, his father, now the reigning monarch, having done so as a midshipman, and the Prince of Wales during his Empire tour in 1920.

H.M.S. *Renown* reached New Zealand on March 22. Auckland went nearly to the point of mobbing the Duke and Duchess with delight. The crowd on the quay broke the police cordon as they landed. Then, as the motor-car procession moved slowly towards the City Hall, swarming people surrounded the Royal car and brought it to a stop.

On leaving Auckland, *Renown* cruised north to the Bay of Islands, one of the loveliest places in New Zealand. The waters here are famous for big-game fish and the Duke during a few days' holiday went out in a launch in pursuit of them. The picture shows him playing a shark which he successfully landed and which weighed 120 lbs.

The Duchess, too, went fishing and, though she did not try for the monsters, she caught twenty fish in half an hour, some of them weighing several pounds. After this pleasant little interlude at the Bay of Islands, the Duke and Duchess struck inland to the thermal region of Rotorua and took up again their schedule of official duties.

The Rotorua district, besides being famous for geysers and hot springs, is the country reserved for the Maori, the native people of New Zealand. The Duke and Duchess are seen here with Sir Apirana Ngata, parliamentary representative of the Eastern Maori at a gathering of the Maoris. They are wearing robes presented to them at the gathering.

A civic reception was held at Palmerston North, the next stopping place of the Royal visitors. While the Duchess was signing the visitors' book, an old inhabitant of the district presented the Duke with a piece of lucky green stone, which he is examining with great interest in the picture. The crowds here were typical of New Zealand's tumultuous welcome.

The tour went on through Napier and Hawkes Bay to Wellington. Here, one of the features was a parade of Scouts and Guides, which is shown above. Just after leaving for the South Island, the Duchess developed tonsilitis and, rejoining H.M.S. *Renown*, was forced to leave the Duke until the New Zealand tour ended and take a complete rest.

The Duke travelled the length of the South Island and, during a visit to Dunedin, went to Otago University. The students gave him a riotous reception and, when he left, hauled his car through the streets. Shortly afterwards, the Duke boarded the ship again at Invercargill, rejoining the Duchess, and the long sea journey to Australia was begun.

Escorted by three destroyers and fifteen aeroplanes, the great battle-cruiser entered Sydney Harbour on March 27. The picture shows her passing between the picturesque Heads of one of the most beautiful harbours in the world. Sydney's whole population seemed to be distributed along the water-front from the landing-stage to Sea Point.

From Sydney, the Duke and Duchess went to Queensland by easy stages. Whenever possible, the Duke visited factories and industrial centres, learning all he could of the industries of the country, but the majority of the time was absorbed by official receptions. This picture was taken as the Duke and Duchess left Maitland, in New South Wales.

During a public reception at Clifton, in Queensland, the Duke and Duchess met Mr. Hendriksen, a Danish settler in the Commonwealth. The old man had been one of the guard of honour many years ago who saluted a Royal bride when the Duke's grandmother, Queen Alexandra, left Denmark to marry King Edward VII of Great Britain.

Outside Brisbane, the railway embankment was lined by crowds for five miles. After an address of welcome at the City Hall, the Duke and Duchess went to Government House. They are shown leaving after the reception. At Beaudesert, they saw a rodeo in which wild cattle were ridden, and Australian aborigines did a terrifying war dance.

While in Queensland, the Duke and Duchess stayed on a station at Tamrookum. The Duke was up early each morning, taking a part in the day's work learning the job of an Australian " squatter." After returning to Brisbane, the motor-yacht *Juanita* took the Duke and Duchess up the Brisbane River through the lovely Moreton country.

Turning back on their tracks, the Duke and Duchess crossed the stormy Bass Strait to Tasmania. They are shown on the steps of Government House, Hobart, during a review of Scouts and Guides. The Governor, Sir James O'Grady, is on the Duke's right. They visited Launceston before the Renown sailed again for Melbourne and the mainland.

The procession to Melbourne Town Hall from the harbour was headed by cavalry. In the picture the procession has halted at the entrance and the Duke and Duchess are about to receive an official address of welcome from the Lord Mayor. A note of tragedy was sounded when two of the escorting aeroplanes collided and four airmen were killed.

The " Sport of Kings " flourishes in Australia. Flemington Race Course is to Melbourne what Ascot and Epsom combined are to London.   The Duke and Duchess went to a meeting on April 23 and saw the race for the King's Cup. The Duke presented the trophy to the winner and is here seen talking to the owner and the winning jockey after the race.

On April 25, the Duke inspected soldiers before a great march past of 25,000 ex-Service men, who had forty V.C.s in their ranks. A commemoration Service was held afterwards in the Exhibition Building. Anzac Day is celebrated each year on the anniversary of the heroic exploits of the Australian Brigade at Villers-Bretonneux on the Western Front.

After the Duke had received the honorary degree of Doctor of Law at Melbourne University, the students ragged him. They took him for a ride round the grounds, made him deliver a speech in the style of a suburban mayor and extracted from him a faithful promise that he would at all times provide beer for less fortunate fellow students of Melbourne.

Now came the mission for which the Duke and Duchess had travelled twenty thousand miles.   Canberra, new-born city of the Commonwealth and the Seat of Government, awaited their arrival. Alighting from a State carriage, the Duke and Duchess ascended the steps of the Parliament Building and here the late Dame Nellie Melba sang the

National Anthem. After an address by Mr. Bruce, the Duke opened the door with a golden key. The picture shows the scene in the Senate Chamber while the Clerk of the Sessions read the King's Commission. The Duke and Duchess of York represented the King-Emperor sitting enthroned while Australian history was being made.

This picture was taken on board H.M.S. *Renown* during the tour.   Before they reached England again, the Duke and Duchess travelled 34,000 miles and went round the world.   They brought a personal note into the attitude towards royalty of distant countries and fulfilled faithfully and ably ambassadorial duties of an invaluable nature in the Empire.

The Duke took exercise whenever possible while at sea on the Australasian tour. He is seen here playing deck tennis with the Duchess against his equerry Major T. E. G. Nugent and the Hon. Mrs. Little Gilmour, Lady-in-Waiting to the Duchess. H.M.S. *Renown* reached England again on June 27 and, after docking, the Duke and Duchess immediately left for London.

King George and Queen Mary, the Duke of Connaught and the Prime Minister greeted the Duke and Duchess at Victoria. There was a brief family reunion at Buckingham Palace, whither Princess Elizabeth had been taken. But on the balcony of their home at 145 Piccadilly, the family waved the greeting that signified they were home at last.

In the middle of July, the City of London offered its greetings and congratulations to the Duke and Duchess on their Empire tour. They drove in state from Buckingham Palace with an escort of cavalry and were received by the Lord Mayor and Sheriffs in the ancient Guildhall. The picture shows the brilliant scene inside Guildhall. The Duke and

Duchess sit on either side of the Lord Mayor, Sir Rowland Blades, afterwards Lord Ebbisham. The Common Serjeant is reading the address, and on his right, Princess Arthur of Connaught, the Prince of Wales, Prince George and the Duke of Connaught can be seen. In the foreground is the double row of Aldermen in robes of scarlet and ermine.

[Photo: Marcus Adams

Though new photographs of Princess Elizabeth had been sent out to the Duke and Duchess in Australasia, nothing equalled the moment of seeing the child again. Eight months old when her parents went away, the baby was now well into her second year and this delightful picture was taken soon after the Duchess returned.

In August, the Duke's scheme to promote a camp for boys from the public schools and from industry was initiated at New Romney, Kent. The Duke spent a very happy day there and the picture shows him returning from a bathing expedition. He joined in a sing-song and made a speech at the camp-fire which was broadcast to the whole country.

On January 29, Earl Haig, Commander-in-chief of the British Forces on the Western Front during the Great War, died in London.   At the funeral procession before the coffin was finally entrained for Dryburgh Abbey, the Prince of Wales represented his father, and the Duke of York and Prince Arthur of Connaught walked on either side of him.

On March 17, the Duchess went to Chelsea Barracks to present the sprigs of shamrock which the Irish Guards wear on that date in honour of St. Patrick.   The picture shows her just after arrival at the Barracks and shaking hands with an officer of the 1st Battalion, Irish Guards, who, including his bearskin, is nearly twice her height.

Royal children are too often seen dressed for public appearance and on their best behaviour.   This refreshing glimpse
of Princess Elizabeth was taken in the garden at her London home, 145 Piccadilly, and shows the little girl having
a game with Princess Mary's younger son, the Hon. Gerald Lascelles, while the nurses are conversing in a group.

When the Duke was on his way to inspect the Royal Marines at Deal, he paused at Sandwich to see some of the
play in the Golf Open Championship.   The picture was taken on the Prince's Course while Walter Hagen, the
famous American golfer, was playing one of the rounds that brought him the coveted Championship once more.

Bearing out his well-known interest in fine horses, King George V visited the Royal Horse Show at Richmond whenever possible. On this occasion, the Duke and Duchess of York arrived first, and the picture shows the Duke greeting his father before they passed into the show ground to inspect the finest bloodstock and the best equipages in the land.

Brilliant weather favoured the Highland Gathering at Braemar this year, which the Royal Family visited from Balmoral. The picture shows their arrival, the figures nearest the camera being, from left to right, Queen Mary, King George, the Duchess of York, the Duke of York. Between the Duke and Duchess is the late Marquess of Aberdeen and Temair

The Duke represented his father and acted as best man at the wedding of the Crown Prince Olaf of Norway to Princess Martha of Sweden. The picture shows the bride and bridegroom with their attendants. On the way to Norway the Duke and Duchess stayed in Berlin for a short while, the first British Royal visit to the German capital since the war.

The research ship *Discovery*, commanded by the explorer, Sir Douglas Mawson, lay in the West India Docks, London, ready to sail for the Antarctic in August. The Duke and Duchess visited the ship in May, accompanied by the Dominions Secretary, Mr. Amery, and are seen going aboard, with the crew waiting to receive them on the foredeck.

Late in May the Duke and Duchess paid a visit to Edinburgh. Prior to a State Dinner, the Key of the City was presented to the Duke. The picture shows him in the full dress of the Queens Own Cameron Highlanders, walking with the Duchess to a service at St. Giles Cathedral during his short stay.

The Duke and Duchess also took part in the celebration of the 600th anniversary of King Robert the Bruce's first Charter to the City. The picture shows the scene at the gateway to the Castle when the Duke unveiled statues of Robert the Bruce and Sir William Wallace, the warrior kings who fought for Scotland's liberty many centuries ago.

The Archbishop of Canterbury and the senior Life Governor, the Duke of Connaught, welcomed the Duke and Duchess when they arrived at King's College, London, in June, for the Centenary celebrations. The picture shows the Duchess walking with the Archbishop to the reception in the Great Hall.

This delightful picture of Princess Elizabeth, now aged nearly two and a half, was taken in the garden at Glamis Castle. Her parents did not spend their usual holiday at Balmoral this year as King George decided not to risk the keener northern air after his serious illness, remaining at Sandringham instead of going to Scotland in September.

The Hon. John Herbert Bowes-Lyon, second son of the Earl of Strathmore, died in February, and was buried at St. Paul's Waldenbury. The Duke and Duchess are here seen arriving at the little country church for the funeral service, which was of the simplest possible character.

Always a keen follower of business house sports, the Duke attended the boxing championships of the Civil Service at the Stadium Club in London on March 27. The picture shows him discussing the progress of a fight with Mr. A. V. Alexander, First Lord of the Admiralty in the then Labour Government.

In the third week of August, the Home Secretary, Mr. J. R. Clynes, was called to Scotland. The Duke and Duchess were at Glamis Castle and the birth of their second child was hourly expected. Mr. Clynes stayed at Airlie Castle, eight miles away, and the picture shows him with the Dowager Countess of Airlie at the local Flower Show.

The new Princess, born in August, was christened on October 30, and is here seen as, with her mother and sister Princess Elizabeth, she was driven to the service. The child was called Margaret Rose and the godparents were the Prince of Wales, Princess Victoria, Princess Ingrid of Sweden, Lady Rose Leveson-Gower, and the Hon. David Bowes Lyon.

[Photo: Marcus Adams

Princess Margaret was the first child in line of succession to the British Throne to be born in Scotland for many years. She was spoken of locally as the 'lassie's bairn,' and the Duke registered her birth at the village shop which combined the offices of registrar, postmaster and grocer.   On the right is a picture of Princess Elizabeth taken at the same time.

[Photo: Marcus Adams

This charming group shows the two children and their mother when Princess Margaret was about five months old and Princess Elizabeth nearly five years.   The infant was looked on rather as a big doll by her sister at first, and then as a possession of which to be proud and of which to talk to visitors.   She called her Bud, because she was a very young Rose.

Royal Ascot took place in kindly weather this year and King George V and Queen Mary with members of their family drove down the course in carriages drawn by the Windsor Greys. The picture shows the Duke and Duchess on the lawns during an interval in the afternoon's racing.

The Duke of York has always been a keen amateur photographer, both with still and moving pictures. He kept a pictorial record of his African tour and of much of the Australasian journey. This delightful snap is from his collection of family photographs, and shows Princess Elizabeth in the garden when a little over four years old.

The Duchess opened the Princess Beatrice Social Centre in Fulham in July. The Centre was for tenants of the Metropolitan Housing Corporation, Ltd. Nearly a thousand people of the tenants gave her a rousing reception. Mr. George Lansbury, then First Commissioner of Works, was present, and the Duchess is seen listening to his speech.

Following the British example, the French Government organised a great Colonial Exhibition in Paris. The Duke and Duchess crossed the Channel to inaugurate a British Week at the Exhibition. This picture was taken at the Morocco Building, and shows the Duchess rather gingerly tasting native sweets after trying the strong African coffee.

[Photo: Lafayette

On August 10, there began at Glamis Castle the golden wedding celebrations of the Earl and Countess of Strathmore. In this family group (above) the Duchess is fourth from the left of the middle row with Princess Margaret on her knee. The Duke is standing behind her, and Princess Elizabeth is on the floor between her grandparents.

On October 24 Lady May Cambridge, daughter of the Earl of Athlone, was married to Captain Henry Abel Smith of the Royal Horse Guards at the parish church, Balcombe, Sussex. Queen Mary, the Prince of Wales, the Duke and Duchess of York and Prince George attended the wedding, and Princess Elizabeth was a bridesmaid. She is seen (left) on the right of the two other little girls, and behind her is Lady Alice Douglas Scott, later Duchess of Gloucester.

[*Photo: Marcus Adams*

Princess Margaret, who had now mastered the difficult art of walking, was, at the time this picture was taken, about eighteen months old and was beginning to take after her mother as regards looks. A tall child for her age, she already showed unmistakable signs of a talent for music which has been encouraged by her parents from the first.

During a tour of the Bolton district in Lancashire arranged for him by the Industrial Welfare Society, the Duke visited several pits. At Gibfield he saw the first pit-head baths erected for miners, and this picture was taken at Atherton Pit before he began a tour of inspection which impressed him greatly. On this occasion he did not descend to the workings.

" Y Bwthyn Bach," Welsh for " The Little House," is inscribed over the door of a model house presented to Princess Elizabeth by the people of Wales. This picture shows the Duke and Duchess at tea in the little house after accepting the gift at Cardiff on behalf of their elder daughter. The house contains six rooms and a hot and cold water system.

Interest in children led the Duchess, in June, to visit Brentwood. At Hutton, nearby, she went to the country branch of the West Ham Central Mission, known as Child Haven. She was photographed as she watched some of the youngsters having the time of their lives in a sandpit.

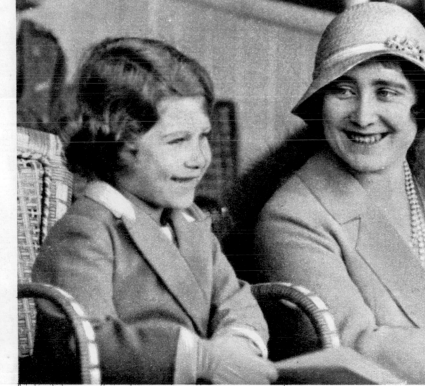

This picture was taken at the dress rehearsal of the Aldershot Tattoo. Princess Elizabeth was one of 40,000 children who saw the pageant, and it is obvious that she enjoyed it, and that her mother was pleased. The success of the day from the children's point of view was the fight between Indians and Pioneers.

While in Scotland, the Duchess visited Arbroath and named the new lifeboat. She boarded the boat and made a tour of the dock. The Duke of Montrose presented her with a silver model of the boat on behalf of the Institution. Here, the Duchess is chatting to veterans of the Lifeboat Service on the quay.

King George ventured to Scotland again this autumn, and his health improved with the change of air. The Royal Family regularly attend Crathie Church when in residence at Balmoral, and this picture of King George and Queen Mary with Princess Elizabeth was taken as they were returning from morning service.

During a two-day tour of factory areas in Nottinghamshire and Derbyshire, the Duke visited the Stanton Ironworks near Ilkeston. He explored the 25-mile area of the works and was specially interested in old and new methods of making iron pipes. The picture shows him chatting to Mr. Sam Page, employed by the firm for forty-seven years.

During a Sale of Needlework and Embroidery done by disabled ex-Servicemen, the Duchess took over a stall and dis-posed of a great deal of stock.   Princess Elizabeth was presented with a petit-point handbag and Princess Margaret with a miniature armchair with a petit-point seat.   The little girls are shown here with their gifts after the presentation.

The Somerset Light Infantry, of which the Duke was Colonel-in-Chief, mounted a guard of honour when the Duke and Duchess visited Bath After a greeting from 5,000 Boy Scouts in the Royal Victoria Park, they made an inspection of the Royal United Hospital. The picture shows a crippled scout presenting the Duchess with a little cradle.

The Duke took every opportunity to talk with the boys at his annual camp and learn something of their lives. This picture was taken at such a moment. Plays, concerts and sing-songs were gradually organised into a regular feature and a big marquee which was specially set aside for entertainments became dignified into the Duke of York's Theatre.

While in Scotland in September, the Duke and Duchess went to the Misty Isle as guests of Macleod of Macleod. The picture shows them landing at Kyleakin, in the south of the Island. In the background is the picturesque ruin of Castle Maol on its rocky eminence. The Duke and Duchess then went to Dunvegan Castle, the ancient stronghold of

the chief of Clan Macleod. This was the first official visit of royal persons to Skye for 400 years and there were scenes of great enthusiasm at every place the Duke and Duchess visited. They opened the new School Hostel at Portree, the capital of the Island, and the Duchess was presented with a gold shawl brooch of ancient Celtic design.

Y Bwthyn Bach.

A charming picture of Princess Margaret and her sister taken outside the little house which was given to Princess Elizabeth by the people of Wales. It stands now in the rose garden at Royal Lodge, Windsor, and the little Princesses spend a great deal of their spare time in it, learning the essentials of running a house in the most pleasant way possible.

The Duke and Duchess took part this year in the Armistice Day ceremonies in Edinburgh.   Contingents of Scottish regiments paraded and the Duke, in the uniform of a Colonel of the Scots Guards, laid the King's wreath on the Stone of Remembrance.   This picture shows the Duke and Duchess in a procession to St. Giles Cathedral for the Service.

[*Photo Marcus Adams*

This year marked the tenth anniversary of the wedding of the Duke and Duchess of York. Princess Elizabeth was nearly eight when this photograph was taken and her sister over three. Recent events have altered the order of precedence greatly and viewed to-day, this charming family group shows the first, third and fourth ladies in the land.

At the end of February, the Duke and Duchess went to Middlesbrough to open a new bridge over the River Tees. The bridge linked the North Riding of Yorkshire with Durham, and cost half a million pounds. The Duke and Duchess, with the Mayor, and followed by many spectators, walked over the bridge after the ceremony of opening.

Like all the Royal children, Princess Elizabeth was introduced to the saddle at an early age. She showed such promise that she was soon able to join the family riding parties at the various country homes. This picture was taken during the course of a riding lesson in the Park at Windsor which contains some of the finest riding country in England.

The Duchess paid one of her many visits to St. Mary's Hospital, Paddington, in April. Three years before she had laid the foundation stone of the new Medical School. She made a tour through all the wards and spent some time playing with and talking to children in one of the nursery wards, a branch of hospital work which specially appeals to her.

The Industrial Welfare Society, of which the Duke has been President for many years, took over new headquarters in Westminster in May. The Duke is seen here examining a number of industrial Safety First posters from other countries which were on exhibition. Under his active guidance, the Society has done valuable work for industry.

[*Photo : Marcus Adams*

Princess Elizabeth was eight years old in April of this year and her sister nearly three and a half. This charming picture shows how Princess Elizabeth takes after her father in looks and Princess Margaret after her mother. Public appearances, carefully regulated, had already endeared both little girls to a vast public always anxious to see them.

The Duke and Duchess of York paid their usual visit to Richmond Horse Show on June 15. A great surprise for the many children present was the unannounced visit of Princess Elizabeth who is seen in the picture on the left affectionately patting one of the winning ponies. She was especially interested in this class of entry.

The Duchess drove through decorated streets during a visit to Sheffield, inspected boy scouts and girl guides and opened the new central Library and the Graves Art Gallery. She is seen in the picture below arriving at the steelworks of Messrs. Firth & Brown where, during her tour of the works, she met 24 employees whose years of service with the firm totalled 1,200 years.

The little Princesses were in great demand at parties given for children in London. They are shown here (*above*) at a fancy dress dance given by Viscountess Astor at her house in St. James's Square. Princess Elizabeth dressed in a shimmering Tudor gown is holding the hand of the little fairy, Princess Margaret.

After a stay at Glamis Castle, the Duke and Duchess and their daughters went as usual to Balmoral this autumn. The little Princesses were taken to the gathering of the Royal Highland Society in Princess Royal Park, Braemar, and are shown comparing notes on the Games with their cousin, Margaret Elphinstone (*centre*).

The Duke and Duchess visited the Mount Pleasant Post Office in November, and the Duke was persuaded to try his hand at sorting mail. In the picture, the Duke, armed with knowledge so recently acquired, is explaining to the Duchess that it's awfully easy, really, while Sir Kingsley Wood, the Postmaster-General, smiles indulgently.

[Photo : Elliott & Fry

On November 29, Prince George, now Duke of Kent, was married to Princess Marina of Greece. The bridesmaids were Princess Catherine of Greece, Lady Iris Mountbatten, Princess Eugenie of Greece, the Grand Duchess Kira of Russia, Princess Irene of Greece, Princess Juliana of Holland, Lady Mary Cambridge and Princess Elizabeth.

The famous Olympia Circus gave a gala performance on January 21 in aid of the South London Hospital for Women. The Duke and Duchess took their daughters to see it and the attraction of the sawdust ring for young and old is plainly seen in this delightful photograph of the family taken during the show.

On April 19, the Duchess of York and Princess Elizabeth were at Westminster Abbey for the distribution of the Royal Maundy. King George V was in his seventieth year and so seventy old people of each sex received the Maundy of £1 plus as many pence as the King was years of age in special Maundy coins which are minted for the occasion.

Perfect weather greeted the Jubilee Day of King George V and Queen Mary on May 6. The Duke and Duchess, with the little Princesses, drove to St. Paul's for Thanksgiving with an escort of Royal Horse Guards. The picture shows them leaving the Cathedral with the Duke and Duchess of Kent. In the background is the Bishop of London.

One of the most moving moments of the Jubilee was on June 9, when King George and Queen Mary and their sons attended in Westminster Hall to receive addresses from the Lords and Commons. The picture shows the Speaker of the House reading the address while the King and Queen sit with two sons on their right and two on their left.

After the London Jubilee celebrations, the Duke and Duchess went north to represent King George V at the Scottish festivities. They stayed with Lord and Lady Elphinstone at Carberry Tower while in Scotland. This picture shows them arriving at a country church for the morning service with the local people assembled to welcome them.

On May 25 the Duke was again in Scotland, and paid a visit to Stranraer. His mission was on behalf of the Carrick Cottage Hospital for which a garden party was held at Castle Kennedy. Children carrying banners with the names of their villages on them brought purses for the Hospital Fund which benefited to the extent of a considerable sum.

In the middle of May, the Duke and Duchess went to the Moorfields Eye Hospital to open the King George V extension. The new building cost £113,000 and was, as the Duke said, "a wonderful tribute to the voluntary hospital system." The picture shows them talking to a little patient during a tour of the whole hospital which they made afterwards.

This great hospital, modernized and re-equipped was ready to begin anew its healing mission on May 29. Nurses provided a guard of honour when the Duke and Duchess arrived, and this picture was taken as a junior probationer presented a bouquet to the Duchess. On the left is Prince Arthur of Connaught, Chairman of the Hospital.

The Duchess of York took the children to see a daylight dress rehearsal of the Aldershot Tattoo. The picture shows Princess Elizabeth greeting the officer of the guard and Princess Margaret just alighting from the car at Rushmoor Arena. 52,000 children were present, and loudly shrilled their welcome.

Foundation Day celebrations at Dr. Barnardo's Girls' Model Village, Barkingside, Essex, were attended by the Duchess of York on June 29. The children gave displays and marched past, prize-winners lining up afterwards to receive their rewards from the Duchess. When she left they obtained flags and formed a guard of honour for her from the door to the road.

Just after the Duke and Duchess returned from a visit to Brussels, a garden party was held at St. James's Palace in aid of the National Council for Maternity and Child Welfare. The Duchess attended and was received by a guard of honour of débutantes. When children presented purses, this little boy took care that his bow should be unmistakable.

For one week each year, the Royal Navy becomes an entertainment centre simultaneously at Portsmouth, Devonport and Chatham.   It opened this year on August 4, and the Duke of York went to Portsmouth to inaugurate the week. The picture shows him as he opened the Navy to the public, speaking from the starboard cathead of Nelson's flagship,

Victory, now in permanent dry dock at Portsmouth. With him is Admiral Sir John Kelly, Commander-in-Chief of the Home Fleet. More than 11,000 people came during the day, the features of the entertainment being submarine operations, shanty singing and crossing-the-line ceremonial and the daily routine of fighting ships in peace-time.

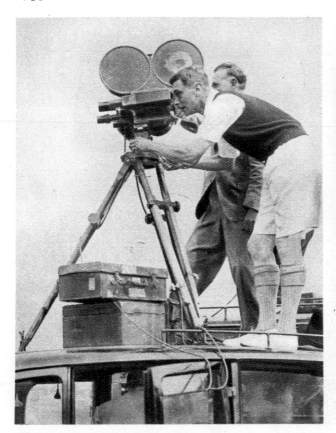

While in camp at Southwold this year, the Duke took 700 feet of film on the cameras of news companies. The picture on the left shows him during the "shooting." The right-hand picture was taken during a march past. of the Black Watch, the regiment of the Duchess's home county, when they received new colours at Glamis Castle.

The Annual Dinner of the Caledonian Society of France took place in November in Paris, and the Duke and Duchess were guests of honour. A large flag bearing the St. Andrew's Cross covered a wall behind the Chairman. The Duke is at the head of the table in the foreground. The Duchess is on the right of Sir George Clerk, the British Ambassador.

King George V, of whom a portrait is inset, died on January 20. After the lying-in-state at Westminster Hall, the coffin was brought in procession to St. George's Chapel for the last rites, a moment shown in this picture. King Edward can be seen on the steps with the sad figure of his mother as the Guardsmen carry the coffin into the chapel.

The Duke of York's elder brother, Edward, Prince of Wales, now acceded to the throne under the style of Edward VIII. Known and loved for so many years as "The Prince," no more popular man ever became King, a fact which heightened the tragedy of events less than a year later. The picture shows him at work in his office suite at St. James's Palace.

At the beginning of March, the Duchess had recovered from severe influenza and went with her family to Compton Place, near Eastbourne, to recuperate. This was the same house where King George V spent several holidays during his last years. In the picture, the Duke and Duchess and the little Princesses are leaving Eastbourne Parish Church.

At Beaconsfield, in Buckinghamshire, there is a model village, perfect in every detail, and known as " Bekonscot."
Princess Elizabeth and Princess Margaret were taken to see it during April, and the picture of Princess Margaret (*left*)
shows her watching the running of the village railway.   Princess Elizabeth is using her height to look down chimneys.

In July the Duke went on a tour of Royal Air Force stations with his brother, King Edward VIII.   They went by car
to Northolt Aerodrome and then flew to Wittering, Mildenhall, Martlesham, and lastly to Hendon.   The picture shows
King Edward looking into a plane at Martlesham while the Duke, in the new Royal Air Force forage cap, stands below.

On the first day of the Court going from full to half mourning, the Duchess opened Coram's Fields and Harmsworth Memorial Playground. They represented the triumph of efforts to save the old Foundling Hospital site for the children, and are now the finest playgrounds in London. The Duchesss is here talking to kiddies playing in the sand-pit.

The Duchess paid her annual visit to the Lord Roberts' Memorial Workshops for Disabled ex-Servicemen in October. It was a surprise visit, and her sister, Lady Rose Leveson-Gower, and the Princesses went with her. The picture shows Princess Elizabeth signing the visitors book and the Duchess coaxing Princess Margaret to do the same.

The scene in Whitehall on Armistice Day was watched by Queen Mary, the Duchess of York and the Duchess of Gloucester. When the Service ended, they were joined by the Princes and walked to the steps leading down to St. James's Park. The picture shows the family coming down the steps with Queen Mary on the arm of her eldest son.

The left-hand picture shows the scene inside Usher Hall when the Duchess received the Freedom of Edinburgh. Almost from this day, events leading up to the crisis began to move swiftly. The Duke and Duchess of York made their last public appearance at the Empire Theatre (*right*). On the night of December 2, they were summoned to London.

What would King Edward do? In trains, in offices, far out at sea, in every corner of the Empire, people discussed the grave news in deep anxiety. While opinions often differed, this unprecedented crisis in British constitutional history was faced with dignity and calm. Here is a typical crowd that waited in Downing Street to see the Cabinet Ministers.

Through the week-end of December 5 and 6 the public waited in anxiety. The comings and goings of all personalities taking part in the drama were followed with intense interest. King Edward remained in the seclusion of his lovely home, Fort Belvedere (*above*) and gave audience to the Prime Minister who is shown (*inset*) leaving No. 10 Downing Street.

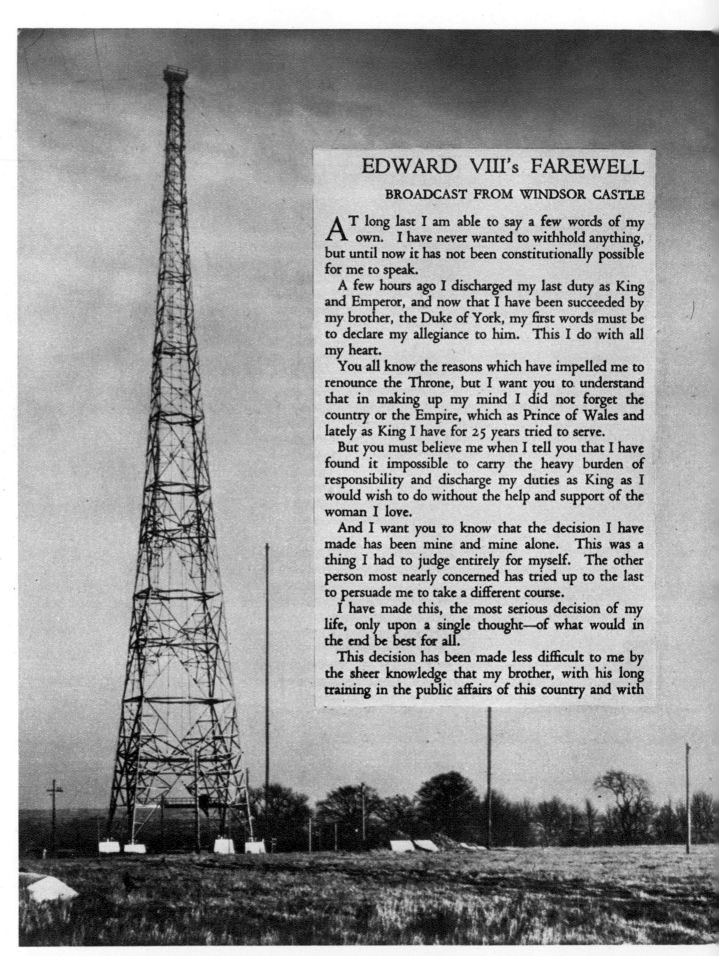

EDWARD VIII's FAREWELL

BROADCAST FROM WINDSOR CASTLE

AT long last I am able to say a few words of my own. I have never wanted to withhold anything, but until now it has not been constitutionally possible for me to speak.

A few hours ago I discharged my last duty as King and Emperor, and now that I have been succeeded by my brother, the Duke of York, my first words must be to declare my allegiance to him. This I do with all my heart.

You all know the reasons which have impelled me to renounce the Throne, but I want you to understand that in making up my mind I did not forget the country or the Empire, which as Prince of Wales and lately as King I have for 25 years tried to serve.

But you must believe me when I tell you that I have found it impossible to carry the heavy burden of responsibility and discharge my duties as King as I would wish to do without the help and support of the woman I love.

And I want you to know that the decision I have made has been mine and mine alone. This was a thing I had to judge entirely for myself. The other person most nearly concerned has tried up to the last to persuade me to take a different course.

I have made this, the most serious decision of my life, only upon a single thought—of what would in the end be best for all.

This decision has been made less difficult to me by the sheer knowledge that my brother, with his long training in the public affairs of this country and with

Reproduced above is the historic last message of Edward VIII, the King who was never crowned. It was the final word before the curtain was rung down on the Crisis. Many millions heard the message, for it went out to Britain, the Empire and the world over the network of the British Broadcasting Corporation. Coming at ten o'clock at night, it was

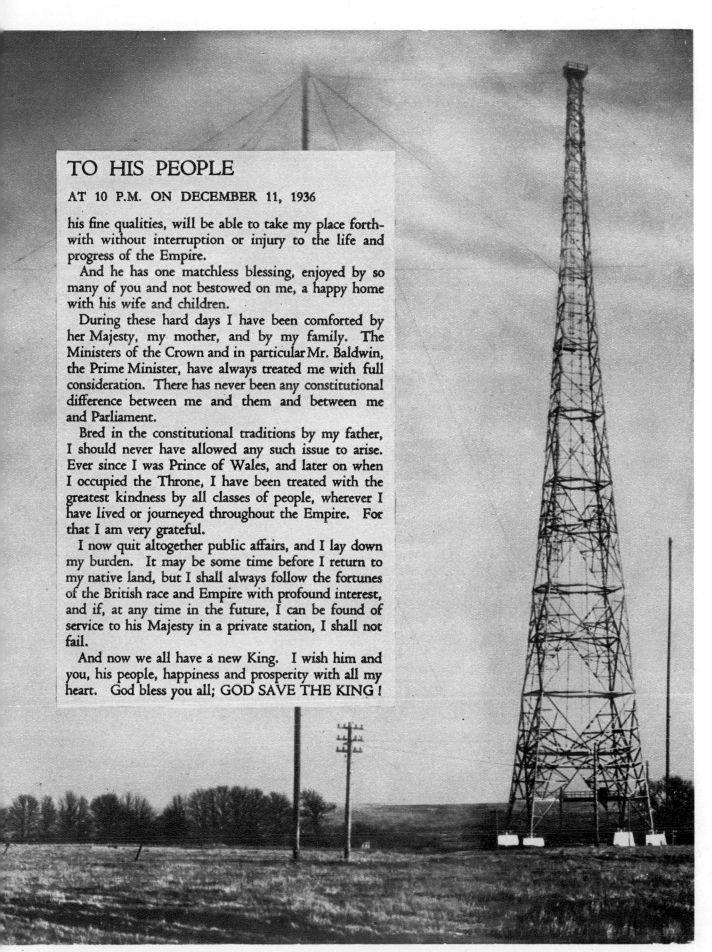

TO HIS PEOPLE

AT 10 P.M. ON DECEMBER 11, 1936

his fine qualities, will be able to take my place forth-with without interruption or injury to the life and progress of the Empire.

And he has one matchless blessing, enjoyed by so many of you and not bestowed on me, a happy home with his wife and children.

During these hard days I have been comforted by her Majesty, my mother, and by my family. The Ministers of the Crown and in particular Mr. Baldwin, the Prime Minister, have always treated me with full consideration. There has never been any constitutional difference between me and them and between me and Parliament.

Bred in the constitutional traditions by my father, I should never have allowed any such issue to arise. Ever since I was Prince of Wales, and later on when I occupied the Throne, I have been treated with the greatest kindness by all classes of people, wherever I have lived or journeyed throughout the Empire. For that I am very grateful.

I now quit altogether public affairs, and I lay down my burden. It may be some time before I return to my native land, but I shall always follow the fortunes of the British race and Empire with profound interest, and if, at any time in the future, I can be found of service to his Majesty in a private station, I shall not fail.

And now we all have a new King. I wish him and you, his people, happiness and prosperity with all my heart. God bless you all; GOD SAVE THE KING!

re-broadcast at theatres, cinemas and dance halls so that all the people should participate in one of the most poignant moments in English history. In the grey hours of the following morning, the farewell was complete when Edward, Duke of Windsor, left his native country and one of the shortest reigns in English history was brought to an end.

On the afternoon of that memorable Saturday in the early hours of which Edward VIII had paid a silent farewell to his country, Prince Albert, Duke of York, was proclaimed in London and throughout the Empire as the new Sovereign, King George VI. In this picture, the Lancaster Herald, Mr. A. G. B. Russell, is reading the Proclamation of the new King at Charing Cross.

Next Monday, December 14, was the King's 41st birthday, and certainly the most notable in living memory. By the King's own wish, there was no official celebration, but the usual royal salutes were fired at noon in Hyde Park and the Tower of London. A family luncheon party was held at which Queen Mary, the Princess Royal, the Duke and Duchess of Gloucester, Princess Alice and the Earl of Athlone were present.

England is fortunate in her Queen Mothers. For fifteen years, Queen Alexandra gained the nation's affection in that capacity. Now Queen Mary takes the title on the same basis. Her experience and her practical wisdom will prove invaluable to her second son in the kingship which he has assumed and form a link between her own reign and her son's.

[*Photo : Bertram Park*

The Duke of York ascended a throne to which, in his mother's words, he had been " summoned so unexpectedly and in circumstances so painful." The Court Circular from Buckingham Palace read : " The Royal Assent was given at 1.52 p.m. to-day to His Majesty's Declaration of Abdication Bill." King George VI's reign dates from that minute.

[*Photo : Bertram Park*

Known and loved by the people since her marriage nearly fourteen years earlier, the Duchess of York, Consort of
Britain's new monarch, brought to the throne a venerated name, one of the proudest in history.   The new Queen
is wife to a man respected by his own peoples and by the world, and she is the mother of two popular little princesses.

In her eleventh year, Princess Elizabeth became heir presumptive to the throne which her father had just ascended. This portrait (*left*) shows the charm which has endeared her to millions of people. The youngest member of the family, Princess Margaret, aged six and a half years, is in the right-hand portrait taken at about the same time.

After a period of incessant business, much of which was concerned with the Coronation, the Royal Family was able at last to leave for a quiet Christmas at Sandringham. The picture shows the King and Queen, with the two Princesses, leaving for the holiday. It is the hope of all that, from a sad beginning, their reign will become a long and happy one.

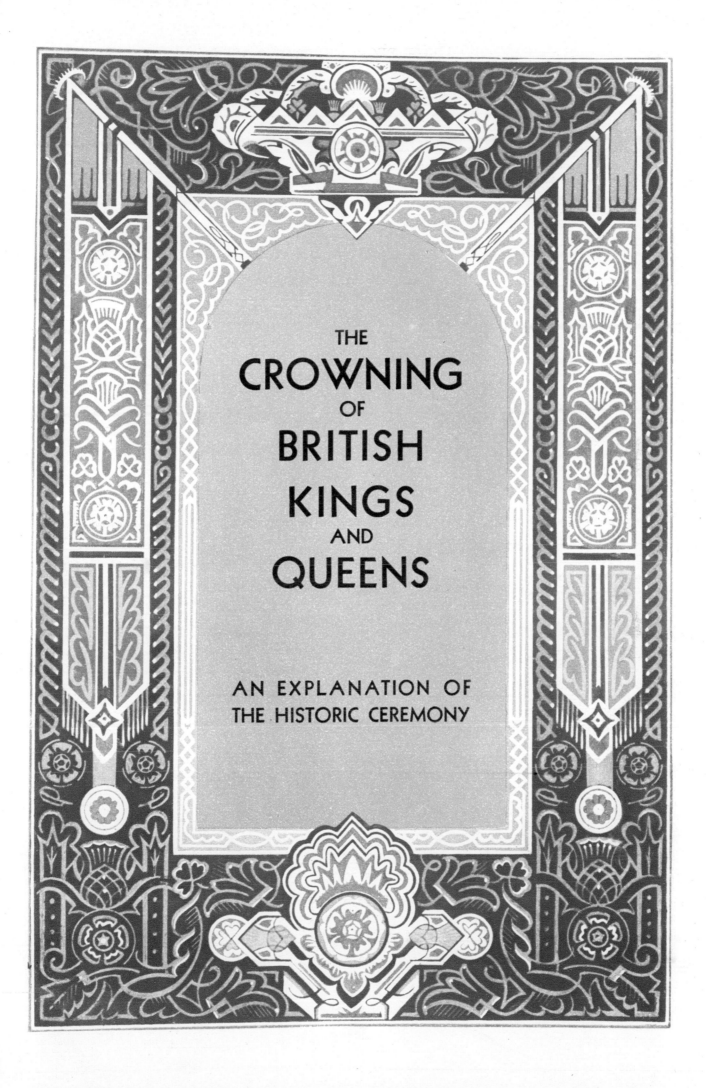

THE CROWNING

OF

BRITISH

KINGS

AND

QUEENS

AN EXPLANATION OF
THE HISTORIC CEREMONY

CORONATIONS THROUGH THE CENTURIES

ON May 12th, 1937, within the walls of that ancient sanctuary, Westminster Abbey, the seal will be set on the Kingship of George VI with all the splendour and solemnity of coronations in days gone by.

The origins of the Coronation, with its elaborate ritual and gorgeous pageantry, are of great antiquity. Britain possesses the oldest coronation service in the world, going back in unbroken continuity to the eighth century A.D.

In pagan Europe, Kingship implied little more than elected leadership for war. The "King" was chosen from among the wisest and bravest men of the tribe. After election, he was raised on a shield and carried three times in solemn procession round the assembled tribesmen. At the end of this ritual a spear was placed in the King's hand, and his brow was bound with a strip of fine linen.

This pagan ceremonial endured for centuries with very little alteration. But after the conversion of Europe to Christianity newly elected Kings received the blessing of the Church, and a religious service was added to the traditional military ceremony. It followed that in the minds of the people the King was endowed with divine protection and something more. Because of it both he and his family were regarded in a new light, and it is not difficult to see how both the hereditary principle and the doctrine of the Divine Right of Kings arose.

The British people, however, never wholly forgot the elective principle of Kingship. This principle, based on the old pagan customs, entitled the people to some voice in deciding which King they wished to have, and how he should behave. Charles I, however, by insisting on the Divine Right of Kings, involved the country, in 1646, in a terrible civil war.

Nevertheless, the idea of the spiritual origin of Kingship had taken strong root. Until as recently as the accession of George I, in 1714, it was widely believed that the King had the power to heal disease by touch. This belief in the power of a King to heal was founded in the ritual of his coronation. A King is anointed with holy oil, and it was by virtue of this anointing that he was credited with such powers.

Thus arose the ancient custom which required the King to "touch" for scrofula—the disease itself became known as the King's Evil—and for centuries British subjects availed themselves of the privilege. Queen Anne even touched that old sceptic, Dr. Samuel Johnson. In England the belief was reinforced by the conviction that English sovereigns were descended from Edward the Confessor, whose holy life had won him a saint's crown and whose reputation for miraculous powers became phenomenal after his death.

Reverence for this saintly King has persisted even to this day. It will be within the walls of the Abbey Church at Westminster, to the building of which the Confessor dedicated his life, that George VI and Queen Elizabeth will be crowned. The Abbey is his church, and there his ghost has watched the solemn coronation of English sovereigns since his body was laid to rest within its walls.

(*By courtesy of the British Museum*)

The Coronation of Edward I.

Some of our Kings, including William the Conqueror, have been crowned twice, and some have delayed their coronations for one reason or another until long after their accession : but all of them, with the exception of Edward V and Edward VIII, have been crowned in the Abbey at some time during their reigns.

William the Conqueror, whose first ceremony on Christmas Day, 1066, was rudely disturbed by an outbreak of fire at the Abbey door, had himself crowned a second time, with his wife, Queen Matilda, on May 11th, 1069. Henry II, after his first coronation on December 19th, 1154, was also crowned again with his queen at Worcester in 1170.

The great Richard I, Coeur de Lion, was crowned for a second time at Winchester after his return from the Holy Land—partly to assert his authority over his brother, John, who had played the King too much for Richard's liking during the latter's absence on Crusade.

Henry III was first crowned at Gloucester on October 28th, 1216, and his mother's bracelet had to play the part of the crown. At the time of his accession Westminster was in the hands of the French, and it was not until 1220 that Henry was crowned in the Abbey.

The Coronation of William I, the Conqueror, was seriously interrupted by an outbreak of fire at the door of Westminster Abbey, a scene shown in the reproduction above. William I was twice crowned, for he went through the ceremony again with Queen Matilda three years later. Another monarch who was crowned for a second time was Henry II.

Queen Eleanor, wife of Henry III was crowned in 1236. Claims to perform the duties at her coronation were so conflicting and numerous that a special body was set up to adjudicate on them. Later, at the coronation of Richard II, in 1377, this body was formally established as the Court of Claims. It still exists and functions, and all those nobles or others who claim the privilege of performing duties at the coronation, whether by right of heredity, by right of attachment to some title, or by right of grand serjeanty (i.e., when the claimant holds lands by virtue of performing certain personal services to the sovereign) must first submit their petitions to the Court of Claims.

A King who was Never Crowned

Edward V, one of the tragic Princes in the Tower, was never crowned. His reign lasted only two months, for he was murdered in 1483, it is said by his uncle, who succeeded him as Richard III.

Henry VII, who was proclaimed King at Bosworth Field in 1485, was crowned at Westminster on October 30th of the same year. This was the first occasion on which a King was proclaimed before his coronation : up to this time the reigns of all Kings had been dated from their coronation. From Henry VII onwards, every King was held to succeed on the death of his predecessor.

Charles I's coronation was marked by three incidents which many considered to spell ill-luck. As a compliment to his wife, whose name was Marie, he had chosen Candlemas Day (February 2nd, 1625), the feast of the Purification of the Virgin Mary. At the last moment, however, Marie refused to be crowned at all.

Secondly, King Charles I decided to wear a white doublet in place of the customary red doublet worn by English monarchs at their coronations. From this fact he is known to history as the White King. And lastly, the royal barge conveying him from the City to Westminster (he chose to go by water instead of in the customary procession) missed the landing-steps and the ill-fated King, with his courtiers,

A picture of the Coronation of Richard II, son of the Black Prince, who was crowned in 1377. This beautiful contemporary picture is reproduced from one of the illuminated manuscripts of the French historian Froissart.

was compelled to scramble ashore in the mud.

His son, Charles II, while still an exile, was first crowned in Scotland at Scone parish church in January, 1651. His formal crowning took place at Westminster on April 23rd, 1661, after his restoration.

During the Commonwealth all the regalia, with the exception of the Spoon and the Ampulla, had been destroyed by agents of the Puritan Parliament and Charles II was obliged to order a complete new set. This set was manufactured by the royal goldsmith, Sir Robert Vyner, whose bill amounted to over £32,000. Inventories of the original regalia existed and the new set was made with careful attention to the original designs, although it did not reproduce them exactly.

James II, who was crowned in April, 1685, had the coronation service amended, and, being a Roman Catholic, refused to receive the sacrament of Holy Communion. It was an unfortunate gesture, for the only other English sovereign who had not received the sacrament was the unlucky King John. But worse was to follow. It was found that the crown would not fit King James's head, and all efforts to make it stay on failed. Henry Sidney, Keeper of the Robes, stepped forward and offered to hold it in place, with the remark that "this is not the first time our family has supported the Crown." At that very time the hypocrite was writing treasonable letters to William, Prince or Orange. Finally, the King's champion, advancing to pay homage in Westminster Hall, slipped and measured his length on the floor.

The Coronation of William and Mary, in April, 1689, was greatly delayed, for the poor queen was perturbed by a letter in which her father, James II, had invoked curses on her head. Fear of the exiled Stuart kept away many of the nobles who should have attended, and the joint ceremony was even more mournful than the coronation of Henry V, which had been carried out in a snow storm.

A King's Ordeal

Queen Anne was so paralysed by gout that she had to be carried to and from her coronation in April, 1702. Another monarch who had been carried from the Abbey was the boy King Richard II, who was crowned in 1382 or 1384. The length and detail of the service was prodigious, and the young King Richard fainted at its conclusion. He was carried back to the palace by his knights.

One of the most elaborate coronations ever staged was that of George IV, in July, 1821. It is estimated to have cost nearly a quarter of a million pounds, and a vast additional expense was incurred because the King refused, after the event, to return the many jewels which he had hired for the occasion.

A sensational incident marked the ceremony. George IV's wife, Queen Caroline (from whom he had been parted for many years) having announced

A contemporary picture of the blessing being pronounced after the Coronation of Henry IV. Coming to the throne in 1399, Henry IV was the first of the three Lancastrian kings of England, and his reign lasted for thirteen years.

The scene in Westminster Abbey at the Coronation of James II in 1685. James's stormy life before accession culminated in an unpopular reign. After the failure of Monmouth's rebellion, an invitation was sent to William of Orange to take the crown and, in 1688, James fled to France, where he died after thirteen years of exile, an embittered and lonely man.

her intention of attending the service, presented herself at the Abbey and made three attempts to enter by different doors, each time being refused admission.

William IV almost dispensed with a coronation. When he went to dissolve his first parliament he took the crown and placing it on his own head, declared to the Lord Chancellor: "This, my Lord, is my coronation day." He was, however, officially crowned on September 8th, 1831.

At the banquet which followed his coronation, the services of the King's champion were dispensed with for the first time for centuries, and have never again

"deny or gainsay our sovereign lord, the King."

As that part of the Coronation ceremonial which once took place in Westminster Hall has in recent times been abandoned, the King's champion is no more.

The right to the office of King's champion is still held by the Dymoke family, in whom rests the lordship of the manor of Scrivelsby, and Mr. Frank Dymoke made claim to the title at the Coronation of Edward VII, in 1902. The Court of Claims recorded his claim, but disallowed it on the ground that since the office was exercised only in Westminster Hall, it had fallen into disuse. Edward VII,

The Coronation Banquet of George IV in Westminster Hall, 1820. This was the last occasion on which the King's Champion performed his office of challenging to combat any who should "deny or gainsay our sovereign lord."

been revived. The office of champion was created as an hereditary right by William the Conqueror, but the earliest record of the actual performing of the office relates to the coronation of Edward III, in 1326, when the champion, Sir John Dymoke, greeted the young King as he emerged after the ceremony, from the Abbey Door.

The Office of King's Champion

In early times the champion gave his challenge and accompanied the King in procession to the Abbey, but later it became customary for the champion to make his first appearance at the banquet held in Westminster Hall after the service. Armed in mail, and accompanied by his shield-bearer, his sword-bearer and heralds, the champion would ride into the hall and throw down his gage to all who should

however, granted Mr. Dymoke the privilege of bearing the Royal Standard of England at his coronation.

The theory of English law is that the heir to the throne succeeds instantaneously upon the death of the sovereign and that the throne is, therefore, never vacant. For this reason, the ceremony of coronation is not actually necessary but is a confirmation and recognition of the new Sovereign and his right of accession. It formally establishes the rights which the people claim from the King in return for their allegiance to him. Parliament does not dissolve upon the death of the King and must meet immediately if the death occurs during an adjournment or prorogation. If the Sovereign dies during a dissolution, the old Parliament is called upon to meet and may serve for a period of six months.

THE CORONATION OF KING GEORGE VI and QUEEN ELIZABETH

CHIEF responsibility for the organisation of the Coronation ceremony falls on the Earl Marshal of England. This ancient office is hereditary in the family of the Duke of Norfolk, the premier duke of England. His first task is to arrange the date of the Coronation, and when this is approved by the King it is proclaimed according to ancient ceremonial, by the Officers of the College of Arms (or Heralds' College) of which the Earl Marshal is the head. The Proclamation, in the present case, was made on December 12th, 1936.

The College of Arms was constituted in the fifteenth century, and is the sole authority in England on behalf of the Sovereign in all matters relating to

all the high officers of State who take part, of their specific duties.

Under his control also are the preparations which have to be made in Westminster Abbey. For this purpose he instructs the Office of Works ; and the First Commissioner of Works, co-operating with the Abbey authorities, becomes responsible for the arrangements.

Another of the Earl Marshal's functions, since it is his right to issue all orders relating to coronations, is to confer with the Archbishop of Canterbury and other high ecclesiastics and with them agree upon the order and form of procedure within the Abbey down to the last detail. Finally, he has to draw up the constitution of the processions, to decide the route

The Duke of Norfolk, Earl Marshal of England.

Sir Gerald Wollaston, Garter Principal King of Arms.

Pedigree, Arms, Honours and similar subjects. Its officers, after the Earl Marshal, are, the three Kings of Arms, Garter (first and principal), Clarenceux (for East, West and South of the Trent), and Norroy (for North of the Trent), six Heralds and four Pursuivants. It is the task of the College of Heralds, acting through the Earl Marshal, to allot and issue all the seats in the Abbey.

Another body with which the Earl Marshal is connected, in his official capacity, is the Court of Claims. This body, which to-day exercises all the powers once enjoyed at coronations by the Lord High Steward, is appointed from certain members of the Privy Council under the leadership of the Lord Chancellor. It receives and adjudicates on petitions from all those who, by one right or another, claim to perform certain duties at the coronation.

When the final awards of the Court of Claims have been made, the Earl Marshal is required to notify all persons to whom rights have been granted, as well as

which will be followed, and to ensure the arrival of all functionaries in good time. For such a brilliant function as a coronation, coaches and carriages are extensively used in preference to motor-cars, and many peers possess State Coronation carriages. It is interesting to note that only members of the Royal Family are permitted more than two horses to their carriage during State ceremonies.

The State Coach, in which the King and Queen drive, was made at a cost of £7,000 for George III's coronation in 1761. Built of oak and weighing over four tons, it is magnificently furnished and bears on its panels allegorical paintings executed by the artist Cipriani.

First to leave the gates of the Palace in the Royal Procession is a staff officer leading an Advanced Guard of a Sovereign's Escort of Life Guards. They are followed at a short distance by the King's Barge Master and twelve Watermen, who precede a number of Dress Carriages and Pairs carrying members

THE CORONATION COACH

This magnificent vehicle was made for the Coronation of George III in 1761. It is constructed of oak throughout, weighs four tons and cost £7,000. The painted panels all round the lower part were executed by Cipriani.

of the Royal Family and certain great dignitaries. Behind ride Aides-de-Camp to the King, Officers of the Headquarters Staff and Marshalmen.

Next appear twenty-five Yeomen of the Guard, followed by the King's Equerries, after whom ride detachments of Colonial cavalry. Then, after a short interval, comes the First Division of the Sovereign's Escort of Royal Horse Guards directly in front of the State Coach carrying the King and Queen. It is drawn by eight cream-coloured horses, four of which carry postilions.

Four grooms walk on either side, and a Yeoman of the Guard at each wheel, while two Yeomen attend each door. Gold Stick in Waiting is on one side of the Coach, the Captain of the Yeomen of the Guard on the other.

The Royal Standard is borne immediately behind the Coach, the Captain of Escort riding on the left of the Standard Bearer and the Field Officer of Escort on the right.

Behind them follow a number of high officers such as the Master of the Horse, the Captain-General of the Royal Archer Guard of Scotland, Equerries in Waiting to the King and Queen, and the Chief Staff Officer ; then the Royal Grooms and, finally, the Rear Division of a Sovereign's Escort of Royal Horse Guards and the Reserve Squadron of Life Guards.

From Buckingham Palace, the Royal Procession passes down the Mall and through the Admiralty Arch into Trafalgar Square. Then by way of Whitehall, Parliament Square and Broad Sanctuary it reaches the West Door of Westminster Abbey.

On the return journey, the route is longer. Leaving the West Door, it passes by way of Broad Sanctuary and Bridge Street to the Victoria Embankment, which it follows until it turns up Northumberland Avenue into Trafalgar Square. From there it proceeds by way of Pall Mall, St. James's Street, and Piccadilly to Piccadilly Circus, where it turns left up Regent Street to Oxford Circus and continues down Oxford Street as far as Marble Arch, and, passing through the Arch into Hyde Park, follows the East Carriage Road to Hyde Park Corner. Passing in front of St. George's Hospital, it continues down Constitution Hill and so back again to Buckingham Palace.

The Regalia of England

The Regalia of England is a narrower term than the Crown Jewels of England. The Regalia proper consist only of those objects such as the Crowns, Sceptres, Orbs, Spurs, Ring and the Swords which are used during the Abbey Ceremony. In early times the Regalia were kept in the Pyx Chapel in Westminster Abbey, but from the reign of Charles II they have been kept in the Tower of London between coronations and are there exhibited to the public. On the eve of King George VI's and Queen Elizabeth's Coronation, the items of the Regalia will be handed over by the Keeper of the Jewel House (the official custodian of the Regalia) to the Dean of Westminster, who will be responsible for their safe keeping until the ceremony is finally completed.

THE CEREMONY IN THE ABBEY

ALTHOUGH the Coronation service to-day is of very much shorter duration than was the case at one time, it still lasts nearly four hours and inevitably imposes a severe strain on the King and Queen.

What may be described as the first act of the formal ceremony in the Abbey takes place on the morning of the day appointed for the coronation. The oil for the anointing having been made ready—it is prepared from the purest olive oil mixed with fine scents and balsams according to a seventeenth-century recipe—it is poured into the Ampulla which, together with the Spoon, is placed on the High Altar and is there consecrated by the Archbishop of Canterbury.

These two objects, the Ampulla and the Spoon, are amongst the oldest and most interesting of all the items of the regalia. The Spoon is, by most authorities, held to be quite the oldest item in the collection; made of silver gilt and set with four pearls it is beautifully chased; almost certainly it dates from the thirteenth century.

The Ampulla is also very old. It is a flask in the form of an eagle with outspread wings, standing upon a pedestal and is made of gold throughout. The head unscrews to receive the oil, which is poured out through the hole in the beak. Its origins are obscure and legends surround them. According to these legends the Virgin Mary appeared to St. Thomas Becket while he was at Sens, in France, and gave to him the Ampulla together with Holy Oil for the anointing of English Kings. For a time the Ampulla was lost, being hidden at Poitiers, but was then discovered by the Black Prince and brought to England. Placed in the Tower of London and again forgotten, it was finally brought to light by Richard II, about 1380.

Certainly the Ampulla is old enough to date back to his reign, though its legendary history may be questioned. It appears to have been kept with the Spoon, in the Abbey, rather than with the rest of the regalia in Westminster Hall, and

because of that escaped destruction at the hands of the Parliamentarians. It was probably found by Sir Robert Vyner when he was making the new regalia for Charles II. By him it was considerably altered. The eagle's wings and the pedestal on which it stands were added, as was most of the chasing which covers it.

The Ampulla and the Spoon are the only two items in the regalia which are placed in the Abbey before the arrival of the King and Queen. The remainder accompany their entry.

The royal procession, having arrived at the West Door, is greeted by the great officers of State, the high ecclesiastics who perform the coronation and those nobles appointed to carry the regalia. As soon as Their Majesties alight from their coach a solemn procession is formed.

This procession is one of the most brilliant and impressive features of the whole ceremony. The gorgeous robes worn by the peers, nobles and high ecclesiastics are surpassed only by the magnificent vestments of the King and Queen themselves and the fires of colour struck from the Crown Jewels of England.

The order of the procession is complicated, and the people in it are numerous. Besides the high dignitaries who take part in the ceremony, there are Heralds, Pursuivants and Officers of the Household as well as many of the Great Officers of State. Each one of the more eminent personages is attended by his pages.

The first part of the procession is made up mainly of high church dignitaries and their attendants. Amongst these are, in order, the Dean of Westminster, the Archbishop of York and the Archbishop of Canterbury. Then follow peers and others bearing the items of the Queen's regalia. Immediately behind comes the Queen herself. She wears a dress of white and silver brocade richly ornamented with pearls, and over it a mantle and tunic of purple velvet lined with ermine. Her long train is carried by six

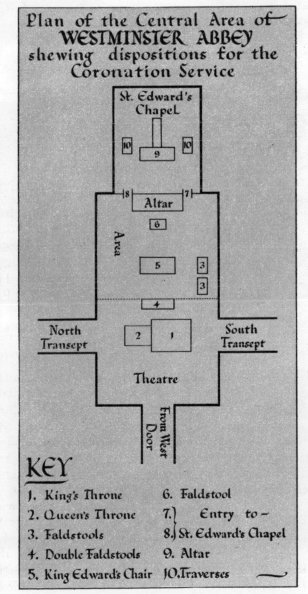

Plan of the Central Area of
WESTMINSTER ABBEY
shewing dispositions for the
Coronation Service

St. Edward's Chapel

10   9   10

8   Altar   7

6

Area   5   3
             3

4

North Transept   2   1   South Transept

Theatre

From West Door

KEY
1. King's Throne
2. Queen's Throne
3. Faldstools
4. Double Faldstools
5. King Edward's Chair
6. Faldstool
7.) Entry to —
8.) St. Edward's Chapel
9. Altar
10. Traverses

Westminster Abbey, one of the finest Gothic buildings in the world, is erected upon portions dating from the Saxon and Norman times. The west towers shown in the picture were designed by Wren and completed in 1740. The clock on the left-hand tower is remarkable for having one long straight hand which points correctly to the hour only.

young ladies (the daughters of earls), and Her Majesty is attended by the Mistress of the Robes. Amongst her immediate retinue are the Bishops of Oxford and Norwich, whose privilege it is to attend the Queen Consort at her Coronation.

The King's Regalia

After the Queen has entered the Abbey the King's Regalia follows. The pieces are borne by peers, each of whom is attended by his page, walking two or three abreast. In the last rank is carried St. Edward's Crown. Behind that follow the Bishop of London (in the centre) bearing the Bible, the Bishop of Winchester (on his right) bearing the Chalice and the Bishop of Ely (on his left) bearing the Paten.

Then comes the King. His Majesty, who is robed in white satin breeches, a crimson tunic and a crimson mantle lined with ermine, enters the Abbey wearing his Cap of Estate (also of crimson velvet), his train borne by six peers and two Pages of Honour. He is attended by the Master of the Robes and the Groom of the Robes. Behind him follow High Officers of the Royal Household and other great dignitaries and the rear of the procession is brought up by twenty Yeomen of the Guard.

Their Majesties are received as they enter the West Door of the Abbey with the anthem "I was glad when they said unto me" (Psalm cxxii, verses 1 to 4), and while it is sung walk down the Nave covered, according to custom, in blue carpet, and passing the thrones (1 and 2) (see plan on page 165), which are set on a Dais built in the centre of the Theatre at the crossing of the Nave and the North and South Transepts, kneel at faldstools (3 and 3) placed before Chairs of Estate on the south side of the Altar.

Reciting the Recognition

Their devotions ended, they seat themselves in their Chairs and the Archbishop of Canterbury, accompanied by a number of high dignitaries, proceeds to recite the Recognition (which presents the King to his people and formally calls upon them to signify their willingness to accept him) from the four corners of the Theatre. During the recital the King stands up and shows himself to the people at each corner in turn.

The scholars of Westminster School, by right of long-established custom, lead off the burst of loyal acclamations with cries of "God Save King George." The acclamations are ended by a fanfare of trumpets.

One after another the pieces of the regalia (with the exception of the Swords) beginning with the Bible, Chalice and Paten are now delivered up to the Archbishop by the Bishops and peers who are carrying them, and by him handed to the Dean of Westminster, who places them on the High Altar.

The King then removes his Cap, and two Bishops, kneeling at a Faldstool (4), placed before the Altar on the east side of the Theatre, intone the Litany. This is followed by the ante-Communion service, the Introit being Psalm v, verse 2, the Epistle I Peter ii, 13, and the Gospel (the same as that which was used at eighth-century coronations) St. Matthew xxii, 15.

A short sermon follows delivered by the Archbishop of York, during which the King replaces his crimson velvet Cap. He hears the sermon seated on his chair (3). The Queen is also seated on her chair (3) on his left.

When the sermon is concluded, the Archbishop of Canterbury rises to administer the Oath. On his accession, a monarch is required to make a Declaration and to swear an Oath. It is the general practice that the King signs the Declaration either at his coronation or at the opening of Parliament, whichever event is first. In it the King declares that he is a faithful Protestant and that he will "according to the true intent of the enactments which secure the Protestant succession to the Throne . . . uphold and maintain the said enactments. . . . according to law."

Taking the Oath

The Coronation Oath is virtually a confirmation, in an extended form, of this Declaration. The Archbishop first asks the King whether he be willing to take the Oath, and on his signifying his assent puts it to him in the form of a series of questions to each of which the King answers separately, demanding if he will swear to govern the people of his commonwealth according to their laws and customs ; if he will cause law and justice in mercy to be executed in all his judgments ; and if he will maintain the laws of God, the true profession of the Gospel and the Protestant Reformed Religion as established by law, and preserve inviolably the settlement of the Church of England and the doctrine, worship, discipline and government of it.

During the solemn silence which follows, the King rises and, assisted by the Lord Great Chamberlain and preceded by the Sword of State, advances, uncovered, to the High Altar. Kneeling before it, he lays his right hand upon the Holy Gospel in the Great Bible which is tendered to him by the Archbishop, and in this posture takes the Oath, afterwards signing the parchment on which the words of the Oath are set down. He then returns to his Chair (3). Both King and Queen kneel at their Faldstools while the Archbishop begins the "Veni Creator." The Hymn ended, the Archbishop offers a short prayer. This is followed by the choir singing the anthem "Zadok the Priest" (1 Kings i, 39, 40), the glorious music for which was specially composed by Handel for the coronation of George II, in 1729. On rising the King is disrobed of his Crimson robe by the Lord Great Chamberlain and, having removed his Cap of Estate, seats himself in King Edward's Chair (5), which has been placed in position before the High Altar.

In this chair every English sovereign since the time of Edward II, with three exceptions, has been crowned. Edward V, one of the Princes in the

The Royal Box is on the left and, in front of it, are the Recognition Chairs. The Thrones of the King and Queen are on the dais on the right of the picture and, in the foreground, are the Faldstools. Between the pillars are the Peers' seats.

Tower, was murdered before he could be crowned. Mary I was crowned on a chair specially sent her by the Pope. Edward VIII abdicated before his coronation.

The chair itself is historic ; yet it is the Stone of Scone, to house which the chair was made, that is the real emblem of antiquity. Its history is surrounded by legend, but whatever its remote origins, it is known that the Stone of Destiny (as it is sometimes called) was placed in the Abbey of Scone by King Kenneth of Scotland in the year 850 A.D., and was used for the crowning of Scottish Kings for centuries.

An Historic Chair

Edward I, who called himself the Hammer of the Scots, caused the Stone to be sent to England in 1296, when it appeared that he had won a final and decisive victory over them. The chair in which it is placed was made by the painter, Master Walter, for the sum of 100 shillings. It is of solid oak, pinned together, and was originally richly carved, but has been severely mutilated through the centuries by irresponsible vandals who have cut their initials in its timbers.

Except during a coronation, when it is placed in the Theatre of the Abbey, it stands adjacent to St. Edward's shrine, and throughout its long history has left the Abbey walls but once. This was on the occasion of Oliver Cromwell's inauguration as Lord

Protector, when the chair was carried into Westminster Hall for the ceremony.

When the King is seated in the Chair, four Knights of the Garter hold above his head a rich silken pall. The Dean of Westminster, having taken the Ampulla and the Spoon from the Altar, pours out a little of the Holy Oil, and the Archbishop, dipping his fingers into the Spoon, anoints the King in the form of a cross on the crown of the head, the breast and the palms of both hands.

Kneeling at a Faldstool placed before King Edward's Chair, the King receives the blessing of the Archbishop and then reseats himself while the four Knights of the Garter return the silken pall to the Lord Chamberlain.

After the blessing the Dean of Westminster robes the Sovereign in the Colobium Sindonis (comparable with a bishop's rochet), a sleeveless garment of fine white linen, and the Supertunica, a long close coat with wide sleeves, bound by a broad girdle.

When the King is robed, the Dean lifts the Great Spurs from the Altar and hands them to the Lord Great Chamberlain, who, kneeling down, touches them to the heels of the Sovereign. They are then returned to the Altar. The Ritual of the Swords now follows.

Five swords are in use at a coronation. The first, the Sword of State, is sheathed in a splendid scabbard of crimson velvet. It may be described as the official sword of England, for it is borne before the Sovereign on all State ceremonial occasions. The next three are all similar in design and in status: they are carried before the Sovereign, upright and naked. The first in dignity is officially called Curtana, or the Sword of Mercy—for which reason it is unpointed. This sword is shorter than the other two, some six inches having been broken off the blade during its history. The second, the Sword of Spiritual Justice, is obtusely pointed, and is borne on the right of Curtana: the third, the Sword of Temporal Justice, is sharply pointed, and is borne on the left.

The fifth sword is known as the Jewelled Sword of State, or the Sword for the Offering and, although it lacks the precise status of the others, it plays an important part in the service. It will be remembered that the Swords are not placed on the Altar at the beginning of the proceedings with the other pieces of the regalia. All except the Sword for the Offering, which is carried on a cushion by the Keeper of the Crown Jewels, are borne by peers who stand on the West Side of the Theatre behind the Sovereign.

When the Great Spurs are returned to the Altar, the peer holding the Sword of State delivers it to the Lord Chamberlain, by whom it is placed in the traverse of St. Edward's Chapel (10). In return the Lord Chamberlain hands to this peer the Sword for the Offering. He in turn passes it to the Archbishop, who, having laid it upon the Altar while he says a short prayer, places it in the King's right hand. The Lord Chamberlain then girds it upon His Majesty.

Redemption of the Sword

After a short prayer the Sovereign rises, ungirds the sword and "offers" it to the Church by laying it, still in its scabbard, on the Altar. It is at once redeemed according to established usage, for the sum of 100 shillings, by the peer who previously bore the Sword of State, and is carried by him naked with the other three swords during the remainder of the ceremony.

The Master of the Robes now delivers to the Dean the Armilla or Stole worn over the tunica, and the Imperial Mantle or Pall of Cloth of Gold, a magnificent garment shaped like a cape, being four square and fitting on the shoulders. The Dean proceeds to invest the King in these garments and the Lord Great Chamberlain buckles the clasp

of the Mantle. Thus arrayed, the King receives the Orb with the Cross: brought by the Dean from the Altar is presented by the Archbishop.

This part of the ceremony is a mixture of the secular and of the religious, for while the Orb signifies dominion, the Cross under which it rests emphasises the fact that all earthly Kingdoms are held under the empire of Heaven. When the Archbishop has pronounced a blessing, the Orb is returned to the Altar, and the Primate, having received the Ruby Ring from the Keeper of the Crown Jewels, thereupon places it upon the fourth finger of the Sovereign's right hand.

The Wedding Ring of England

The putting on of the ring signifies the union of the sovereign with his country and the ring is, in consequence, frequently referred to as the "wedding ring of England." A story is related of Queen Elizabeth that when pressed by the Commons to marry, she pointed to the ring on her finger and answered that England was her husband and Englishmen her children.

By ancient right, the Lord of the Manor of Worksop (the Duke of Newcastle) now presents a right-hand glove which the Kings puts on. The Lord of the Manor of Worksop is now entitled to support the Sovereign's right arm when the Sceptre with the Cross is delivered by the Archbishop into the King's right

The Coronation Chair.

171

The Most Rev. His Grace the Lord Archbishop
of Canterbury.

hand. At the same time the Primate gives the Sceptre with the Dove into his left hand; the former is the emblem of Kingly power and state, the latter of equity and mercy.

All the ceremonial preliminary to the actual crowning is now completed and the Archbishop, standing before the Altar, solemnly consecrates the Crown known as St. Edward's. This crown, made by Sir Robert Vyner in 1662 to replace that destroyed by the Parliamentarians, is believed by most authorities to be a fairly exact replica of the one worn by Edward the Confessor, and thereafter used in coronations up to the time of Charles I. Described as the Official Crown of England, it is made of gold richly embellished with a multitude of precious stones.

When the consecration is concluded, the Dean of Westminster, assisted by other bishops, raises the cushion on which the crown rests and follows the Primate to King Edward's Chair.

Crowning the King

Lifting the crown in both hands, the Archbishop reverently places it upon the King's head. At once the peers and the Kings of Arms put on their coronets, a fanfare of trumpets breaks the solemn silence and again the scholars of Westminster School lead the acclamations of the assembled people, "God Save the King." Outside the Abbey the multitudes take up the cry which is caught and carried from street to street. Through the deafening cheers echo the thunders of the great guns at the Tower of London booming out their salutes. A new King is crowned.

As the cheers within the Abbey die away, the Choir begins its singing of the glorious anthem "Be Strong and Play the Man." When it is ended, the Dean of Westminster approaches the Sovereign and

presents the Bible; the King delivers it back to the Archbishop, who then proceeds to the Benediction.

Next follows the Inthronization. The Sovereign rises from King Edward's Chair (5) and, approaching the Dais, is assisted into his throne (1) by the two Archbishops, the Bishops, and other peers. In the old days the phrase "lifted up" was used to describe this part of the ceremony, for it was related to the pagan custom of raising the new King on a shield borne by his chief men.

Now, in solemn array, the Great Officers of State, the Peers who carry the Regalia, and the Nobles carrying the Swords, group themselves around the steps of the Throne while the Archbishop prays that the King will "stand firm, and hold fast from henceforth the seat and state of royal and imperial dignity."

Rendering Homage

The Archbishop is the first of the King's subjects to render Homage. All the Bishops kneel in their places while the Primate kneels before the Throne and renders his fealty, speaking for himself and for them. He is followed in order of precedence by the Princes of the Blood Royal being peers. Then the other peers, putting off their coronets, kneel down in their places rank by rank in order, dukes, marquesses, earls, viscounts, and barons. As each rank kneels, so the senior member of that rank advances to the Throne and pays Homage for himself and for his Order. Those who pay their Homage in person at the knees of their Sovereign touch the Crown on rising and kiss his left cheek. During the Homage the choir sings the anthem "Rejoice in the Lord."

When all Homage is paid, the drums beat and the trumpets sound, and new acclamations break from the assembled people.

The Most Rev. His Grace the Lord Archbishop
of York.

1, St. Edward's Crown; 2, Imperial State Crown; 3, The Sword of State; 4, The Sword of Spiritual Justice; 5, The Jewelled Sword; 6, The King's Orb; 7, The Queen's Orb; 8, The Sword of Mercy or Curtana; 9, The Sword of Temporal Justice; 10, The Chalice; 11, The Paten; 12, Sceptre with Dove; 13, The Royal Sceptre; 14, Spurs and Coronation Ring; 15, Ampulla and Spoon; 16, St. Edward's Staff; 17, Rod of Equity; 18, State Crown of Queen Mary.

Edward the Confessor, King of England from 1041 to 1066, was canonised by the Church a century after his death. To the building of Westminster Abbey he devoted most of his life and much of his original planning still remains in the existing edifice. This picture shows The Confessor's shrine, behind the High Altar, where his remains lie.

All is now ready for the Coronation of the Queen. This ceremony, though naturally far shorter than that for the King, is equally dignified and impressive. It must be remembered that the wife of a King is only a Queen Consort and not a Sovereign in her own right. Her Coronation, which sets a seal upon her Queenship, is designed partly to define her status in relation to that of the King to whom she, as much as any other person in the British Empire, owes allegiance.

Anointing the Queen

For the first act of the ceremony the Queen, supported by two Bishops, kneels before the High Altar, and after prayers have been said walks to the Faldstool (6) set between the steps of the Altar and the Dais, directly in front of King Edward's Chair. The ceremony of her anointing follows closely that of the King. Four Peeresses hold a rich pall of Cloth of Gold over her while the Archbishop anoints her on the crown of the head. After the anointing the Archbishop, having received from the Keeper of the Jewel House the Queen's Ring, places it upon the fourth finger of her right hand. This ring is set upon her finger as a seal of sincere faith.

The actual crowning of the Queen Consort again follows closely in procedure that of the King. The Queen's Crown, which rests on a cushion and has been placed with the other items of the Regalia upon the High Altar, is brought by the Dean of Westminster to the Archbishop who, lifting it from its cushion, reverently places it upon the Queen's head. The act of Crowning is the signal to the Peeresses in the Abbey to put on their coronets. The Queen then receives from the Archbishop in her right hand the Sceptre with the Cross, and in her left hand the Ivory Rod with the Dove. Carrying these, she rises and moves towards her Throne (2) set on the Dais. As she passes in front of the King seated upon his throne on the Dias, she bows.

The King and Queen being now crowned, the Communion Service follows. Their Majesties deliver their Sceptres to the Peers who previously bore them, advance to the steps of the Altar and remove their Crowns, which they deliver to the Lord Great Chamberlain. They then kneel reverently at faldstools placed side by side, in front of the Altar.

The King's Oblation

The King, receiving from two Bishops Bread and Wine brought from St. Edward's Chapel, offers them to the Archbishop. Thereafter the Sovereign makes an oblation of a pall or altar cloth handed by the Officer of the Great Wardrobe to the Lord Great Chamberlain and by him, kneeling, to His Majesty; and of an ingot or wedge of gold of one pound weight, delivered by the Treasurer of the Household, also to the Lord Great Chamberlain who, as before, passes it to His Majesty.

A similar oblation is made by the Queen, who offers a pall or altar cloth and an ingot of gold of a mark weight. The Primate places these gifts on the High Altar and, the King and Queen having passed to their chairs (3 and 3), proceeds with the Communion Office.

After the Primate, the Archbishop of York, the Dean and Bishops have communicated, the Sovereign and the Queen Consort again advance to the Altar and receive from the Archbishop the bread on the Paten, and from the Dean the Wine in the Chalice.

When they have communicated, they return to their Thrones, put on their Crowns and receive back their Sceptres. Prayers and the singing of the "Te Deum" by the choir conclude the Service.

The Procession is now re-formed: the Archbishop takes the items of the Regalia from the High Altar and hands them to the Peers appointed to carry them, and the Sovereign, preceded by the four Swords carried upright and naked, passes into St. Edward's Chapel by the door (7) on the south side of the Altar. Similarly the Queen passes into St. Edward's Chapel by the door (8) on the north side. The King there delivers his Sceptre with the Dove to the Archbishop, who lays it upon the Chapel Altar (9) together with other pieces of the Regalia, such as the Spurs and St. Edward's Staff, surrendered by the Peers who carry them.

He is then disrobed of his Imperial Mantle and arrayed in a Robe of Purple Velvet. St. Edward's Crown is taken off his head, and in its place he puts on the Imperial Crown.

The Imperial State Crown

It is this Crown which is carried before the Sovereign on all State occasions. It was made by the order of Queen Victoria in 1838, and was embellished with jewels taken principally from older Crowns; the chief of them is the famous Ruby in the centre of the Cross patée, said to have been given to Edward the Black Prince by Don Pedro, King of Castile, in the year 1367, and later worn by Henry V in his helmet at the battle of Agincourt in 1415.

The Crown has been rebuilt for successive Monarchs. When it was remade for Edward VII, the smaller of the two larger portions of the famous Star of Africa diamond (weighing over 309 carats) was built under the Cross. As it exists at present, the Crown contains nearly 300 pearls and some 2,820 diamonds.

Bearing in his right hand the Sceptre with the Cross, in his left hand the Orb, and wearing the magnificent Imperial Crown, the Sovereign passes out of St. Edward's Chapel. His procession is joined in the theatre by that of the Queen, who carries her Sceptre in her right hand and her Ivory Rod in her left. They walk slowly in solemn procession down the nave of the ancient Abbey through the galleries packed with bowing spectators, to emerge from the West Door into a roar of cheering—the crowned King and Queen of the British Commonwealth of Nations.

The Editors gratefully acknowledge their indebtedness for much of the above information to the Publishers of Debrett's.

The choir-stalls are in the foreground and far back is the high altar. Between the choir and the altar the solemn ceremony of coronation is carried out. Here, in one of the world's most famous churches, for many centuries, the Kings and Queens of England have come to their crowning, and now the scene is set once more for the ancient pageant.